How to play DOUBLE BOGEY GOLF

How to play DOUBLE BOGEY GOLF

THE ART OF BEING BAD AT A GREAT GAME

HOLLIS ALPERT,
IRA MOTHNER,

and

HAROLD C. SCHONBERG

TIMES BOOKS

RANDOM HOUSE

Library of Congress Cataloging-in-Publication Data
Alpert, Hollis.
How to play double bogey golf: the art of being bad
at a great game/Hollis Alpert, Ira Mothner,
Harold C. Schonberg.
p. cm.
ISBN 0-8129-1869-X
1. Golf—Humor. I. Mothner, Ira.
II. Schonberg, Harold C. III. Title.
PS3551.L7H6 1990
796.352'0207—dc20 89-77473

MANUFACTURED IN THE UNITED STATES OF AMERICA

9 8 7 6 5 4 3 2

SECOND EDITION

BOOK DESIGN BY GUENET ABRAHAM

CONTENTS

PREFACE

OUR ANCESTORS KNEW. They knew that what a man was born to he would remain all his life. Don't struggle. Accept things as they are. Your reward is in Heaven. In the meantime float uncomplainingly on the choppy river of life, occasionally submerging and gulping huge mouthfuls of water before coming up for air. Such is the way of mankind. Just as some are born to riches and others to poverty, so it has been ordained that some are born with a grooved swing and others—so many others!—require seven strokes to get from tee to green. There is a good reason for that, unfair as it may seem, and our forebears celebrated it in song:

> *The rich man in his castle,*
> *The poor man at his gate,*
> *God made them high and lowly*
> *And ordered their estate.*

To paraphrase a more famous line, God must have loved the Double Bogey Golfer because he made so many of them.

Thus, things being ordained, the Double Bogey Golfer, staggering from rough to rough, blundering into bunkers, shanking every second short iron, whimpering over his fourth putt, has a place in the great order, like a hyena, the coelacanth, the mosquito, and the wood tick. He still remains one of God's creatures, though he remains more perplexed than most of them about the fitness of things. Why are such humiliations visited on *him*? To a man of his character, intellectual endowments, and financial stability? To a man of his overwhelming talents? To a golfer of his potential?

But that is how things are. God has indeed ordered the estate of the Double Bogey Golfer. The 34-handicap player may have his visions and aspirations, like Vachel Lindsay's worm who eats the cauliflower yet dreams of higher things. (Listens to the meadowlark and wonders how it sings). Deep within himself, Mitty-like, he *feels* the powers that strain to be unleashed. Somewhere within him is the secret combination that, once figured out, will make him the possessor of the picture swing, the mighty breaker of par. But— complicated creature—on a deeper level below *that* he knows such things will never be, that he is what he is.

If the Double Bogey Golfer is wise, he will adopt the stoicism of Marcus Aurelius. The secret of human life, said old Marcus, is to fathom the general character of the universal order so as to live in harmony with it. Stoicism may, of course, be tempered by existentialism, *à la* Kierkegaard: We are all in despair, consciously or unconsciously. The Double Bogey Golfer, following the teachings of such great philosophers, should learn to accept the universal order that has placed him at a 34 handicap. He will learn to make the best of day-in, day-out series of rounds that in less philosophic golfers would create a commotion in the mind, a perturbation in the spirit, and a confusion of humors and mental juices.

The trouble is, however, that very few Double Bogey Golfers are philosophers. Only too often they struggle against their place in the nature of things. They will not heed the immortal words of the late Senator Roman Hruska of Nebraska about the desirability—indeed, the necessity—of mediocrity.

The Double Bogey Golfer . . . has a place in the great order.

Thus the Double Bogey Golfer takes lessons. He stands on the practice tee until his hands are a lake of blisters. He spends countless desperate hours seeking to correct a slice. (The Double Bogey Golfer seldom hooks; he is almost invariably a slicer.) He purchases new clubs annually. First it was bamboo shafts, then hickory, then steel, then glass, then aluminum, graphite, bronze, titanium, and blendings thereof. With each new set of metal "woods" he is confident that a breakthrough is at hand.

He is always disappointed.

Turning to the golf magazines, he studies them as Saint Francis read the Bible, taking everything as received wisdom (and the prose in golf magazines, especially when describing the physiological increments of actually hitting a little golf ball, can be more impenetrable than the Book of Revelation). Did not Saint Arnold say this? Did not Saint Jack say that? And what is the latest received wisdom from Saints Greg and Seve?

As well try to learn to play the piano like Van Cliburn by reading instruction books.

The Double Bogey Golfer nevertheless builds a golf library, poring over the books in it more carefully than Kasparov ever studied the Dragon Variation of the Sicilian Defense. He practices his putting on the living-room carpet, careful to purchase carpets that have the consistency of closely cropped grass. He stretches a blanket in the backyard and whangs slices into it. Like Sir Lancelot following the Grail (Lancelot did at least get a fleeting vision of it) he puts aside all mundane matters in his unachievable search for the unattainable.

These activities only make matters worse. Nothing helps, nor can it.

So what is a man to do?

Simple.

Buy this book.

It is a very serious study, based on the latest research. In it are revealed secrets through which the Double Bogey Golfer can learn to live with himself, establish domestic tranquillity, achieve a new world view, make golf a pleasure rather than a scourge, and maybe —oh, joyous day—break 100 every once in a while.

This is a book for the Double Bogey Golfer, written by Double Bogey Golfers (or former Double Bogey Golfers) out of vast experience, sympathy, understanding, experimentation, reading, study, meditation, and inner urgency. Our researches have helped us. Our researches will help you.

It takes one to know one.

How to play DOUBLE BOGEY GOLF

INTRODUCTION

UNLIKE ALMOST ALL treatises devoted to the art and sport of golf, this one provides no formula for perfecting the golf swing, nor does it unveil the secrets of putting employed by Greg Norman, Ben Crenshaw, or Curtis Strange.

We live in a real world. For most of the millions of us, playing a round of par golf is as likely as winning a 10 million dollar lottery. It happens, but the odds against it are enormous. The authors spent years of self-loathing, guilt, and deep depression before they reached a sensible and quite revolutionary conclusion.

It came in a flash!

How necessary for us was it really to play in the 70s, the 80s, or even the 90s, to enjoy the game? Could self-fulfillment be reached with a high handicap?

It struck us that something was wrong about the nature of the game for the vast majority of golfers, and we discovered what it was: The scoring system itself!

Here is the heart of the matter. Playing to par is a concept inherently aristocratic in nature and is a throwback to an ancient time. We learned that the antidemocratic nature of so-called par came about during the early history of the game.

Centuries ago, golf began attracting the common people—the sower, the reaper, the blacksmith, the hewer of wood—so much so that royalty became concerned and declared the sport illegal. Anyone caught playing golf in Scotland during the 15th century was fined and imprisoned. King James II, who rammed this law through the Scottish Parliament, was fearful that time frittered away swatting a little ball along a course of grass and gorse would lead to deterioration in archery skills needed for an effective fighting force.

Noblemen were exempted, however, less by fiat than by custom. Their pursuit of the spherical object was winked at, since it was deemed less important for them to hit a bull's-eye (or a vulnerable spot on an enemy) than to command others to do so. Golf was confined largely to the aristocrats. The common folk could only skulk around the seaside pastures and make derogatory remarks about the idle rich.

We can cite here a quite meaningful passage in Tobias Smollett's novel, *The Expedition of Humphrey Clinker,* published in 1771. He wrote of a certain Edinburgh foursome, *"all gentlemen of independent fortunes"* who had amused themselves at the pastime *"for the best part of a century* [italics ours] and achieved a considerable amount of dexterity."

There's the clue. The scoring system was designed for people with enough wealth to play at the game continually. Even after ordinary folk were once more admitted on the courses (the invention and use of gunpowder had much to do with this), the low score was the means whereby the aristocrats and the landed gentry could separate themselves from the hoi polloi. Farmers and herders had little time to take off from their chores, and when they did so they were outclassed by those of independent means. Strangely, Karl Marx failed to mention class distinctions in golf in his *Communist Manifesto.* If he had done so, he would have made his point with greater ease. For surely seeds of the class struggle are to be found in that early separation of aristocrats and plebeians—pars on the one hand, outlandish scores on the other. A proletariat of golf was born long before Marx conceived of his notion.

Marx's lapse (and Engels's, too, for that matter) explains why golf was neither invented nor taken up by the Soviets—that is, until recently, when Mikhail Gorbachev and the Communist party decided to revise Marxian socialism along more democratic and capitalistic lines. (China played with the idea for a time, too.) But until he came along with his *glasnost* and *perestroika,* the Soviets regarded golf as an imperialist and decadent recreation. A good many authorities now predict that when golf is more widely played in the Soviet Union, Marxism-Leninism will be a dead duck. This book, with its liberal and democratic point of view, should be welcomed by Comrade Yeltsin in the Soviet Union; and if only in the interest of peace and harmony and the foreign trade balance, a good many copies should be shipped there as soon as possible.

Revisionism in the form of the bogey came to golf coincident with the Industrial Revolution in England and elsewhere. There are those who still regard bogey golf as an opiate for the exploited working class; others see it as a bone tossed to the military and the defense industry. Indeed, "bogey" took its name from the colonel who was also father to the well-known march tune. Bogey arrived late at the game, but he played well and managed to average only a stroke a hole above par. As a consequence, the 1911 edition of the Encyclopaedia Brittanica defines "bogey" as "the number of strokes that a good average player should take to each hole."

Well and good. We have no quarrel with bogey golf. If your desire is to excel and you are capable of it, go ahead and do it. What we see, though, is a golfing population that has grown explosively, and to inflict concepts of par and bogey on the entire gamut of golfers is certainly cruel. Let there be no mistake: The occasional golfer is a Double Bogey Golfer. Triple bogey golfers abound, too, but triple bogey golf is not recommended. The courses these days are crowded, and triple bogey golf takes too long to play. We suggest that in the interests of shortened playing time and course maintenance the triple bogey golfer use this book as a guide for stroke and time saving.

Aha! says the skeptic. What about the handicap system? Doesn't it work to equalize unequal abilities? Yes, it does, and it's not a bad system, but it has a serious flaw. Psychologically speaking, it is a disaster. The "scratch" golfer and the 36-handicapper are handed the same printed scorecards with the number of strokes to be taken for each hole. When a golfer exceeds every one of the numbers by two or more strokes, consider the burden of failure he carries by the end of the round!

Millions know the dread feeling that comes when it is time to add up strokes. Some, before they add up the total, crumple the scorecard in disgust. Others don't bother to put down a number for a hole, but simply mark an X in the little box. Here is a scorecard rescued from a trash basket near the 18th green . . . (name omitted):

1	2	3	4	5	6	7	8	9	10	11	12	13	14	15	16	17	18
7	5	x	6	x	x	5	7	x	6	7	x	8	5	5	7	4	x

The above example may seem shameful, but it is not unusual. For millions upon millions the par standard is wrong. Face it. How many play to it? In a recent survey, we collected 734 scorecards turned in at Dreadful Dunes Country Club on a typical weekend. Par for the course was 72. Here are the results:

Par or better:	3
73–80:	17
81–85:	42
86–90:	86
91–100:	107
100–XX:	479

Jokes abound about the situation. You've heard the story, haven't you, of the weekend golfer who scored a 9 for every hole but the 18th, on which he carded a 12. "What happened to you on the last hole?" his partner inquired. "What do you think I am?" the fellow replied. "A machine?"

Millions know the dread feeling that comes when it is time to add up strokes.

Isn't it high time for the great mass of golfers to rise in protest against a scoring system that bears little relationship to the way they play? Does this happen in tennis? No. The scoring system makes the game the same whether played by the most miserable hacker or Boris Becker. Does it happen in any other sport? NO.

Double Bogey Golf is the answer.

Here is the way in our recommended system a printed scorecard should look for anyone whose handicap is 30 or higher:

1	2	3	4	5	6	7	8	9	10	11	12	13	14	15	16	17	18
6	7	5	6	6	8	5	6	6	6	6	5	7	6	6	7	6	5

This scorecard is geared for success, not failure. It is sensible and achievable, a kinder and gentler scorecard. Double bogey par, as we term it, is within reach of the occasional player, the tyro, wives tired of being confined to the bridge table or worried about what their husbands are doing when they say they play golf. It helps the temperamentally unsuited and the muscle-bound—anyone who has been doggedly punishing himself in the pursuit of what we term professional par.

Let that par remain for the beautifully gifted people of golf. Let them continue to expound on the intricacies and theories of the perfect golf swing. Let them use their beryllium copper shafted drivers, their perimeter weighted graphite boron irons (which do nothing at all for the Double Bogey Golfer). Their entire lives being devoted to golf and nothing but golf, let them have *their* par. This book doesn't attempt to put the professional teacher out of business. He will still have plenty of customers. In fact, we of the Double Bogey Golf world can create a whole new class of teachers who will fit the game to the ability, rather than attempting the reverse.

The virtues of Double Bogey Golf are many. The game becomes pleasant and relaxing. Using the above scorecard, the golfer's attitude changes remarkably. No longer will his coronary system be threatened every time he plays. Tensions are notably eased. He has room for error. Error, he comes to realize, is a natural, *fun* part of the game. Watching a pro-am tournament on TV he will smile benevolently and with symbiotic understanding when a movie star or an ex-president dribbles his way to a hole.

An acquaintance of ours to whom the secrets of this book were imparted quit group therapy, finding it no longer necessary. Another lowered his cholesterol level by 50 points in one month. His blood pressure readings returned to normal (in his case, 128/84). The head of a middling-size law firm, he arrived at his office one Monday morning and amazed his staff by his cheery, hearty greetings.

One caution: Regard with suspicion any large improvement in score that comes from reading this book. We don't seek to lower your score, only to make you comfortable with it.

THE DOUBLE BOGEY
GOLFER'S MANIFESTO

"IF GOD HAD meant man to golf," argued Peter Piper the Elder before the Aberdeen presbytery, back when Scotland first sanctioned Sunday sports, "the Almighty would have made man's right side shorter than his left. Thus, he could not but strike the ball out fair and high." Besides using the word "golf" as a verb for the very first time and revealing greater knowledge of the game (if little of kinesiology) than any other 17th-century divine, old Peter put his finger on golfing's number one problem. Few men (and fewer women) are naturally designed to play it well.

Indeed, the "classic" golf swing—that illusory arc, pivot, and push—is perhaps the most unnatural of all athletic movements. God simply could not have intended man to play par golf. If He had, then a perfect swing would be as automatic as the movement of fork to face. Since it is not, golfers must struggle against their divinely programmed inclination to handle a driver as though it were an ax, sledge, or mallet. "Golf," declared Piper's great-hearted contemporary MacTeague, the Sage of Frither Glen, "was sent to test mankind."

The testing can be heard on tee and green, in rough and bunker throughout the land, particularly on warm Sabbath mornings, as golfers rant and bend their clubs in distress, resisting a fate that has nailed their handicaps somewhere north of 20. They resist double bogeydom, their natural condition, for lack of spirit and the strength of character to accept it.

By far the most torturous part of the test is to view without rancor those happy few with perfect or nearly perfect golfing motions. They exist, as do others who can accomplish *pirouettes en pointe* and four-minute miles or traverse Olympian swimming pools, butterfly fashion, in 26 seconds flat. "Many are called, but few to greatness," as MacTeague has said. Only a select number are given the means to control the raising and lowering of their golfing utensils so as to speed balls holeward in booming drives and pitches of majestic precision. Plainly, they are freaks.

Thorvald MacDougal, a high-handicap contemporary of Young Tommy Morris (four times the British Open champion, winning first in 1868), has written wisely on the proper attitude to take toward scratch or near-scratch golfers. "Courtesy, decency and simple right-thinking instruct us to ignore the deformities of others. Yet, good and kindly souls, who would not dream of staring at a cripple or making sport of a midget, will peer and ogle and make a great show over golfers whose skills are so at odds with normal abilities as to be marked eccentric or unnatural." To MacDougal is credited golf's great social doctrine. It was he who said, "All golfers are peers."

If indeed all golfers are peers or equals, then the Double Bogey Golfer is most equal of all. No golf club of 250 playing members can have many more than a score of championship class players and two score of straight bogeymen. Of course, we are counting *every* member—matron, maid, stripling, and codger—and every stroke, not just those the prideful post on their good days. Clearly, the vast majority of golfers follow the Almighty's design and round the course in man's natural relationship to par—double bogey.

This is not badness. It is the golden mean of golf, for the sad truth is that there are subdouble bogey inadequates just as there are near-scratch freaks. Not everyone has the skill and rhythm to break the 110-stroke barrier that is the bottom line of double bogeydom.

It was MacDougal, the first great champion of the "natural" (i.e., high handicap) golfer, who declared: "Let the governance of golf rest with the greatest group of golfers."

Obviously, he was speaking out for his own, raising a challenge to the tyranny of excellence that dominated the game in his day as in ours. Low-handicap golfers have always been a pushy and puffed-up lot. They have never perceived that their abilities do not make them *better* than other players. They make them *different,* strange, queer, peculiar, and certainly unsuitable to determine what is best for all of golfing golfdom.

The authors do not go so far as MacDougal, who considered a low handicap to be as desirable an attibute as wens or warts. We say there is a place for the low handicapper on the course (though they are an impatient crew) and room for them in the clubhouse (boastful and loutish lot though they may be). But there is no more room for them on golf, greens, rules, and tournament committees, save in proportion to their numbers. It is not for such as them to determine the placement of pins, the length of holes, thickness of rough, prizes, pairings, and when winter rules may be played. "We will not," as MacDougal protested, "be ground under the mashies of sweaty semiprofessionals and exhibitionists."

Why have MacDougal's words fallen on deaf ears? Why has not the mass of golfing humanity risen to claim its rightful dominance of the game? It is because the lesson of MacTeague, Sage of Frither Glen, has been lost.

"Golf was sent to test mankind." And we have, thus far, failed the test. We have to a man (and increasingly to a woman) scorned our natural state, struggled to pervert double bogeydom into something rigid and artificial, in direct violation of the Almighty's genius.

The test of golf is not athletic, but spiritual. It is not our game that must improve; it is ourselves. We must be at peace with the duffer within us. Only then will we grow in spirit, and growth of spirit is what golfing is all about.

The test of golf is not athletic, but spiritual.

1   WHAT NOT TO DO

IT TAKES GUTS. It's like kicking cigarettes, booze, and chewing gum all at once. It is like forswearing peanut butter. It is like going off sex. But it has to be done.

Don't read instructions by pros or teaching pros. Or if you haven't got the determination to stop reading them, at least don't take them too seriously. If you do take them seriously, the result is like going to a quack shrink. You'll end up in knots.

It's madness. One pro says your right hand is too strong. The other looks you square in the eye and says it's too weak. One says you play the ball too far to the right. Another says you play it too far to the left. One says you're leading with the shoulders. Another says you're not leading enough with the shoulders. One says the club is overcontrolled. The other says it's undercontrolled. A guy can go crazy reading this stuff.

Fortunately for the Double Bogey Golfer, most of it is as undecipherable as Second Dynasty cuneiform. In the first place, you have to be an anatomist to understand it. In the second place, most anatomists themselves don't understand it. In the third place, those who claim they *do* understand it break a couple of blood vessels laughing over the mistakes. In the fourth place, once a Double Bogey Golfer starts getting himself twisted up with the various contradictory exegeses of the golf writers, he will suddenly find himself a triple bogey golfer or maybe even a quadruple bogey golfer. In the fifth place, it asks the Double Bogey Golfer to perform unnatural acts. In the sixth place, it fills the head with confetti. In the seventh place, it confuses him. In the eighth place, it just doesn't work.

Hard words, you say? Exaggerated, you say? Well—

In an issue of a certain popular golf magazine, a teaching pro tells you how to overcome the six most common faults of the golf player. The first fault is misaiming the club face. The cure: "Draw a straight line to your target and another that intersects the first at right angles. Then practice hitting balls off the first line while aligning the leading edge of your clubface parallel with the second."

Fault No. 2: Playing the ball too far right in your stance. Cure: "Draw the intersecting lines in the turf as described in the previous cure. Place the ball at the intersection of the lines and position your feet so the second line extends to the inner edge of your left heel. Be sure you do not allow your shoulders and thighs to turn open to the left as you place the club head to the ball in its new up-forward position."

Fault No. 3: Right side too high at address. Cure: "Cock your knees laterally toward the target . . . and place about 60 percent of your weight on the inside of your right foot. This tucks the right knee inward. . . ."

And so on, and so on. The cure for Fault No. 5 has an entrancing poetry of its own. Fault No. 5 is leaving the line too soon on takeaway. The cure: "Draw a line straight back from the ball. Then make another line back from 'four o'clock' on the ball (see drawing). Swing the club head back for several inches along the first line, then return it along the second. . . ."

All this is undoubtedly great and good advice written by a great and good man. But its only real value, aside from contributing to

Don't read instructions by pros or teaching pros. . . . The result is like going to a quack shrink. You'll end up in knots.

the gaiety of the nations, is whatever the pro got paid for writing it. Let the Double Bogey Golfer try to put these nuggets of wisdom into effect. Just let him try. His head will be so full of lines, angles, weight shifts, and other impedimenta that by the time he gets up there he's going to *miss* the damn ball.

If, indeed, he can even begin to follow the directions. Ever try putting 60 percent of your weight on the inside of your right foot? I mean, are you *kidding?*

Or what is the Double Bogey Golfer to make of this kind of prose:

> When the right hand is dominant, the grip end of the club is dragged back at the start of the take-away as the club head remains stationary and the left hand is put into a broken or submissive position. In effect a reverse single hinge is created. Harry Vardon and Bob Jones are

examples of top players who used this method.

Equal use of the right and left hands approaches the true "one-piece" theory in which any wrist hinging is inhibited until the player is well into his backswing. Byron Nelson was one of the top players utilizing this method.

There are, according to Toski and Flick, basically three ways to set the angle: (1) a set and swing; (2) a swinging set, and (3) a swing and a set. There are advantages and disadvantages to each, but the pendulum swings in favor of the first two because they get the angle set earlier, forcing the right hand to become more submissive and overpowering. . . .

Once you reach the top, your left side is still in control, your hips and legs must control the forearms and hands into and through the forward swing, maintaining the smooth body flow that helps retain the angle. The left knee works in a lateral rotation toward the left toe, down the flight path and back to the left of the flight path. The right side stays soft and exerts no influence until the left side pulls it into position and centrifugal force brings it into play without any conscious help from you.

Yeah.

The only parallel in the history of human thought to this kind of writing is the long section on the transcendental unity of apperception in Kant's *Critique of Pure Reason*. In the original German, of course.

Forget all this. There is a much simpler way to understand the nature and dynamics of the golf swing. Simply let x equal the right side; y equal the left side; z, the left hand; t, the right hand; a, the right knee; and d, the left knee. The elements of the golf swing are then easily obtained by putting for space of four dimensions the equation for the spherical golf ball:

$$x^2 + y^2 + z^2 + t^2 = R^2 \ldots \ldots (1)$$

and for the distance *ds* between the points (x, y, z, t) and $[(x + dx)$ $(y + dy)\,(z + dz)\,(t + dt)]$ the value

$$ds^2 = dx^2 + dy^2 + dz^2 + dt^2 \ldots\ldots (2)$$

It is easily found by means of the methods used for three dimensions that the shortest lines are given by equations of the form

$$\left.\begin{array}{l} ax + by + cz + ft = 0 \\ \alpha x + \beta y + \gamma z + \phi t = 0 \end{array}\right\} \ldots\ldots (3)$$

in which *a*, *b*, *c*, *f*, as well as *a*, β, γ, ϕ, are constants.

The length of the shortest arc, *s*, between the points (x, y, z, t) and (ξ, η, ζ, τ) follows, as in the sphere, from the equation

$$\cos \frac{s}{R} = \frac{x\xi + y\eta + z\zeta + t\tau}{R^2} \ldots\ldots (4)$$

One of the co-ordinates may be eliminated from the values given in equations 2 to 4 by means of equation 1, and the expressions then apply to space of three dimensions.

If we take the distances from the points

$$\xi = \eta = \zeta = 0$$

from which equation 1 gives $\tau = R$, then,

$$\sin\left(\frac{s_0}{R}\right) = \frac{\sigma}{R}$$

in which

$$\sigma = \sqrt{x^2 + y^2 + z^2}$$

or,

$$s_0 = R \cdot \text{arc sin}\left(\frac{\sigma}{R}\right) = R \cdot \text{arc tang}\left(\frac{\sigma}{t}\right) \ldots\ldots (5)$$

In this, s_0 is the distance of the point *x*, *y*, *z* measured from the center of the co-ordinates.

If now we suppose the point *x*, *y*, *z* of spherical space to be projected in a point of plane space whose co-ordinates are respectively

$$\ast = \frac{Rx}{t}, \; \mathbf{p} = \frac{Ry}{t}, \; \mathbf{z} = \frac{Rz}{t}$$

$$\mathfrak{x}^2 + \mathfrak{y}^2 + \mathfrak{z}^2 = \mathfrak{r}^2 = \frac{R^2 \sigma^2}{t^2}$$

then in the plane space the equations 3, which belong to the straightest lines of spherical space, are equations of the straight line. Hence the shortest lines of spherical space are represented in the system of $x, \mathfrak{y}, \mathfrak{z}$ by straight lines. For very small values of $x, y, z, t = R$, and

$$\mathfrak{x} = x, \mathfrak{y} = y, \mathfrak{z} = z$$

Immediately about the center of the co-ordinates, the measurements of both spaces coincide. On the other hand, we have for the distances from the center

$$s_0 = R \cdot \text{arc tang} \left(\pm \frac{\mathfrak{r}}{R} \right) \ldots \ldots (6)$$

In this, $\mathfrak{r}$ may be infinite; but every point of plane space must be the projection of two points of the sphere, one for which $s_0 < \frac{1}{2} R\pi$, and one for which $s_0 > \frac{1}{2} R\pi$. The extension in the direction of $\mathfrak{r}$ is then

$$\frac{ds_0}{d\mathfrak{r}} = \frac{R^2}{R^2 + \mathfrak{r}^2}$$

In order to obtain corresponding expressions for pseudospherical space, let R and t be imaginary; that is, $R = \mathfrak{R}i$, and $t = \mathfrak{t}i$. Equation 6 gives then

$$\text{tang} \frac{s_0}{i\mathfrak{R}} = \pm \frac{\mathfrak{r}}{i\mathfrak{R}}$$

from which, eliminating the imaginary form, we get

$$s_0 = \frac{1}{2} \mathfrak{R} \log. \text{nat.} \frac{\mathfrak{R} + \mathfrak{r}}{\mathfrak{R} - \mathfrak{r}}$$

Here s_0 has real values only as long as $\mathfrak{r} = R$; for $\mathfrak{r} = \mathfrak{R}$ the distance s_0 in pseudospherical space is infinite. The image in plane space is, on the contrary, contained in the sphere of radius R, and every point of this sphere forms only one point of the infinite pseudo-spherical space. The extension in the direction of $\mathfrak{r}$ is

$$\frac{ds_0}{d\mathfrak{r}} = \frac{\mathfrak{R}^2}{\mathfrak{R}^2 - \mathfrak{r}^2}$$

For linear elements, on the contrary, whose direction is at right angles to $\mathfrak{r}$, and for which t is unchanged, we have in both cases

$$\frac{\sqrt{dx^2 + dy^2 + dz^2}}{\sqrt{d\mathfrak{x}^2 + d\mathfrak{y}^2 + d\mathfrak{z}^2}} = \frac{t}{R} = \frac{t}{\mathfrak{R}} = \frac{\sigma}{\mathfrak{r}}$$

$$= \frac{\sqrt{x^2 + y^2 + z^2}}{\sqrt{\mathfrak{x}^2 + \mathfrak{y}^2 + \mathfrak{z}^2}}$$

Or, as Srinivasa Ramanujan so wittily put it:

(1.7) If $\alpha\beta = \pi^2$, then

$$\alpha - \tfrac{1}{4}\left(1 + 4\alpha\int_0^\infty \frac{xe^{-\alpha x^2}}{e^{2\pi x} - 1}\,dx\right) = \beta - \tfrac{1}{4}\left(1 + 4\beta\int_0^\infty \frac{xe^{-\beta x^2}}{e^{2\pi x} - 1}\,dx\right)$$

2 THE IMPORTANCE OF BEING EARNEST [AND ITS DREADFUL RESULTS]

BUT SUPPOSE A Double Bogey Golfer is so driven that he continues to read the instructions of the professionals and tries to put them into effect. This can lead to certain anfractuosities not envisioned by the great MacTeague and other Founding Fathers of Golf (blessed be their memory).

For whereas the pro and the scratch player know, or pretend to know, all about leg action and wrist angles and left-side-forward and right-side-backward, the Double Bogey Golfer, who has generally started late in life with a pot belly and the strength of an undernourished amoeba, painstakingly has to work out certain elementals for himself.

If he takes the Sacred Writings of the teaching pros literally, that can be a lot of work.

Let's say that he reads that the cure of misaiming a club face (see previous chapter) is to draw a straight line to the target and another line that intersects the first at right angles. The Double Bogey

Golfer, a literal and optimistic sort of fellow, wants to follow this advice. Behold him at every tee with a huge ruler and a pail of whitewash, industriously inscribing lines and right angles. How else can he be sure of not misaiming the club face?

He further has read that 60 percent of his weight has to be placed on the inside of his right foot. Now, the typical Double Bogey Golfer is about five feet, eight inches tall and weighs, say, 200 pounds. That means 120 pounds of this weight must be on the inside of his right foot. But how to follow orders? Can *you* sway and tell when 60 percent of your weight is on the inside of your right foot? Can you?

In fact, the determined Double Bogey Golfer has only one sure way to determine how much weight is on which foot. He goes out and gets a bathroom scale. Even so, most determined Double Bogey Golfers find it rather difficult to swing a golf club with one foot on a bathroom scale. There is, of course, an obvious solution: another bathroom scale. At least balance is achieved, though the double bogeyer must now order clubs four inches longer—which is perhaps a small price to pay even if the clubs have to be hand-made.

A 60:40 weight ratio is one thing, but the Double Bogey Golfer also remembers that several teachers recommend, for fairway woods and irons, 70 percent of the weight on the inside of the right foot. And to complicate matters further, there are those who urge that for short wedges and chip shots 60 percent of the weight be on the *left* side.

What it comes down to, then, is that the Double Bogey Golfer has to hit off scales on every shot. Suppose he hits a chip shot in which only 55 percent of the weight is on the inside of the left foot? That would not be following the instructions, and our seeker after perfection desperately wants to follow instructions. How else can his game improve?

But hitting off scales creates problems. They weigh 6 or 7 pounds at the very least. That means 12 to 14 more pounds for the caddie to tote. The caddie simply won't do it. There is a pro-shop revolution. Or, in those cases where the club does not have caddies (a vanishing species, like the osprey and the $10,000 car), the Double

Bogey Golfer will have to lug the scales himself, a task he finds distasteful.

But nothing will stop him. He works up a contraption akin to the mechanism that attaches skis to the feet. This he welds to the top of the scales. He then attaches spikes to the bottom of the scales, gets his feet into the attachments and lurches down the fairways, happy in the knowledge that he can get exactly 60 percent (or 70 percent if necessary) of his weight on the inside of his left foot on a chip shot. True, he needs some assistance. He cannot *read* while preparing to hit. But what is a partner for? Down on his knees, the partner reads the scales. There is a countdown: "108 pounds . . . 109 pounds . . . 110 pounds, HIT!"

So much for weight. There are angles of pronation to consider. To measure the kind of wrist angles described by the pros, the Double Bogey Golfer can get a sextant or a goniometer. By these means he can focus exactly on Harry Vardon's reverse single hinge. There is an attractive spinoff: He can also focus exactly on that four o'clock line to cure a faulty take-away. A giant-sized protractor is also recommended. For the sextant, a book of trigonometric functions and log tables, a pad, and an electronic calculator are of great assistance.

The Double Bogey Golfer has also been seen with a carpenter's level (the kind with a big bubble) attached to his shoulders. The level is for determining the proper turns.

Furthermore, the highly handicapped, if he pursues his quest to the logical end, also wears blinders, invariably stolen from a Central Park horse. He does not like to steal from horses, but recently blinders have been hard to come by. He wears blinders because he has read that most weekend golfers see too much when they look at the shot facing them; their peripheral vision takes in too wide a view of the hazards on the left and right of the fairway. "Experienced players," says one article, "learn to have tunnel vision, seeing only the area where they want the shot to go." Let people laugh, but blinders work, or so our Double Bogey Golfer insists. Has not a pro said so? So he insists on wearing the blinders. That makes him look even more a horse than nature originally intended.

In his laudable ambition to improve his game, he'll try everything. Sometimes it works, sometimes it leads to trouble. One Double Bogey Golfer once read this headline in a golf magazine: SPRING INTO THE SWING FOR MORE POWER. The article went on to explain: "The legs should spring forward from the top-of-backswing position if they are to be active enough to generate power for your shots. Visualize yourself *springing* off your right instep at the start of the downswing, then twisting your legs and body through the shot, with your weight ending up on your left foot and your right toe acting as a balance point. This would be the reaction of a tautly wound spring once it were released, and this should be your action through the ball."

Out marched our hopeful to the practice tee, muttering the liturgy. He read and reread, then swung like the release of a tautly wound spring. When he tried to pick himself up from the ground, he discovered that his legs had indeed sprung. They were twisted up like a knot of rubber bands, and the femurs had screwed themselves a good five inches into the pelvic girdle.

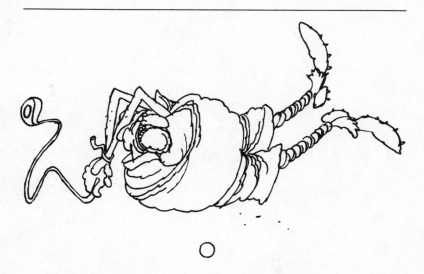

He . . . swung like the release of a tautly wound spring.

The Double Bogey Golfer who takes as gospel the tips from magazines can find other unusual things happening to him. Watson says this, Norman that, Nicklaus something else. Comes the day when a strange figure advances to the first tee. All onlookers regard it with awe. The more superstitious ones cross themselves. This figure has the calves of Mark Calcavecchia, the thighs of Jack Nicklaus, the hips of Craig Stadler, the wrists of Paul Azinger, the shoulders of Severiano Ballesteros, the ankles of Tom Kite, the waist of Ben Crenshaw, and the hands of Curtis Strange.

But when it swings, it immediately becomes all too apparent that it was put together by Dr. Frankenstein.

3 CLASSIC DOUBLE BOGEY SWINGERS

It can be stated authoritatively that no Double Bogey Golfer swings like a par golfer. He has nothing like the swing described in any book of instruction. He reads these books, of course. They are, in fact, his preferred reading matter, and he will pass the long winter priming himself, with words of the masters, for the coming golf season. But, once on the course, his arms, legs, head, and body go their idiosyncratic ways.

Who has not read the great Bobby Jones on the proper golf swing? Surely one of the most familiar of all passages is the following by Jones:

> Many players begin the backswing with a sudden pronation of the left wrist that whips the club sharply around the legs, opening the club face very quickly. This is just as bad as a swing straight back (upright) carrying the arms away from the body. The initial movement of

the club away from the ball should result from forces originating in the left side. The real take-off is from the left foot, starting the movement of the body. The hands and arms soon pick it up. But the proper order at the very beginning is body, arms, and lastly club head. It is always easier to continue a motion than to begin it; this order has the virtue of originating the hip turn; it goes a long way toward assuring a proper windup of the hips during the backswing.

There it is, clear as crystal, the secret of the master golfer revealed. But for the Double Bogey Golfer, Jones might as well be writing in ancient Chaldean. The words just don't translate into action—at least not for him.

Thus, after many hours of instruction, after he has driven thousands of balls off the practice tee, the Double Bogey Golfer inevitably evolves his own swing.

These swings often have great originality, and if one is objective, not inclined toward absolutism, they can make for fascinating study. Vardon, Hogan, Snead, Nelson, Palmer, Armour, Middlecoff, Nicklaus, Watson, and Tewell have all written copiously on the theory and mechanics of the classic golf swing, but never, so far as we know, has anyone bothered to record the theories and mechanics of that far richer form, the Double Bogey swing.

To fill this gap, interviewers with tape recorders and stop-motion cameras were sent into the field—to several golf courses—to capture for posterity the words, and swings, of the most interesting Double Bogey swingers. From among many, three have been chosen for their articulateness and daring.

Pauncho Mayer, age 42, regularly plays the Bad Rock Country Club course at Blackland, Arkansas, where a recent videotape on Double Bogey Golf was made called *Black Day at Bad Rock*. Mayer's handicap recently moved from 36 to 35, an improvement he credits to an individual style 17 years in the making.

His swing can briefly be described as follows: At address he plays the ball some four inches from his right foot. Knees bent deeply, so that they seem about to buckle, and using the interlocking grip with the left hand bent slightly to the right, he draws the club head back swiftly to an upright position, whereupon he pauses for two full seconds. Then, with a leftward body lunge, he brings the club head down in a wide hooking arc across the ball, following through to the left until his right foot rises to follow the club head. At the finish of the swing, he is facing the clubhouse. The flight of the ball thereafter is erratic, but generally flies some 90 to 140 yards away into light (and playable) rough on either side of the fairway.

"Long ago," said Pauncho Mayer, "I threw away my driver and then disposed of the three wood also. I was not getting the results I wanted. I discovered, too, that the R or Regular stiffness of my clubs was too pliable for me, causing me to lose control of the club head at the top of my backswing. I changed to Extra Stiff clubs, which I had especially made for my swing. For driving I use a 3⅞-wood. Now I am getting the results I want. On a par-four hole, I can definitely reach the fringe of the green in, say, three and a half strokes, and if my chipping and putting are working well I can take a six, which enables me to play right around my handicap.

"When I took up golf seventeen years ago I began by swinging in the orthodox manner, using Hogan as my guide. I never managed to get the ball up in the air. I usually topped it 20 or 30 yards and I'll confess that sometimes I missed the ball entirely. Being a methodical sort, I began to experiment.

"You'll notice I'm a bit heavy around the waist, and that my left wrist is a half inch larger than my right. That's because I used to play Ping-Pong with my sister left-handed. I realized I was getting *too* much left hand into the ball and that my waist prevented much of a shift on the follow-through. So I loosened the left hand and let the right hand have more play. Then I experimented with stance. I found the more I played off the left foot the more likely I was to hit on top of the ball, much like a hammer head driving a nail into a board. I kept moving the ball closer to the right foot until I achieved the right spot fairly close to the right foot. Someone pointed out to me that I was swinging stiff-kneed. I tried bending them. The deeper I bent my knees the more likely I was to make contact with the ball. I've been told by a lot of the Bad Rock members that my swing doesn't look right but at least I get off the tee, and I intend to stay with it. I use a low compression ball, by the way, and pink translucent plastic tees."

Tom Zehner, who plays the Rampage Hills Course near Hell Mountain, New Jersey, has a 32 handicap and a swing which others at his club enjoy watching. He stands in a pronounced crouch that reminds one of Mookie Wilson when he played for the New York Mets. In fact, he holds the club much like a baseball bat. The arms go straight back on the backswing. At the completion of the backswing the club describes a menacing little circle, his left foot lifts, his right foot strides forward at the moment of contact with the ball. He has used the same swing for 12 years, scores consistently between 110 and 112, and does well at nassau.

"In my youth," says Zehner, now 65, "I was employed as a shipper at the Artform Corset Company in Trenton, New Jersey. The company had a softball team, and I was the star hitter. I could really smack that ball. I modeled my softball swing on that of Roger Maris the year he hit 61 homers. Eventually, Artform was taken over by Svelteform in Somerville, and I rose to head the shipping department, which gave me time to take up golf. Recently I sold my stock in the company and retired to Hell Mountain, overlooking Rampage Hills. I just couldn't get the hang of the swing. Then I thought: Why not try that old softball swing? Well, the results were simply amazing. I pretended the little ball was not standing still but coming right at me very low and inside. Naturally I teed it high, about five inches off the ground and thwack! the ball traveled on a line 180 yards into the left rough, the direction and line of flight about like that of a baseball or softball going over the shortstop's head into left center.

"Admittedly, the swing required adjustment. I closed my stance and faced a point about 50 yards from the green on the right, in that way getting the ball closer to the middle of the fairway, the idea being to hit over second base instead of the shortstop. Using my swing I can hit the ball a country mile, but I have problems with chipping. The swing doesn't work for that. I was having trouble with putting, too, until I thought of it in terms of bunting. I began laying down bunts, if you'll forgive the figure of speech as applied to golf, and they work fine. I've sunk them from 30 feet away. 'Just get it between the pitcher and the third baseman,' I tell myself. Or, 'Lay it down the first base line.' I set up for a bunt (a putt, I mean) with my regular crouched stance, then slide my right hand down the shaft and stroke. Works fine for me."

Norbert Popkin can be seen on weekends at the municipal course on the outskirts of Danville, Connecticut. Six feet six inches tall, with an elongated neck, he realizes he does not have an ideal golfer's build. Never able to break 120, he went to a series of pros for advice. One advised him to use short clubs because of his very long arms; another advised long clubs because short clubs caused him to bend over like a willow in disconsolation. He finally settled on Cary Weinerblut, a retired tour golfer who had taken up drinking after losing 14 straight tournament play-offs. It was Weinerblut's opinion that club length was not the problem, which lay in other directions. Let Popkin take up the story at this point:

"I signed up with Weinerblut for a winter series of lessons at his practice cage above Sam Gelding's Hardware Store and Power Mower Repair Center. Frankly, I came to suspect that Weinerblut was more interested in Jack Daniels than Jack Nicklaus. I'd be on the rubber mat and he'd sit nearby on a stool, sort of nodding. Each time I swung at the ball he'd merely say: 'Head moved' or 'Head moved again' or just 'Head.' Even when I didn't swing he'd say 'Head.'

"Finally, the message got across. No matter how much I tried to keep my head still, it always moved. I decided to see Dr. Clyde Beguine, an orthopedic surgeon in Danville. I told him about my lack of control over my head during the golf swing. The problem, he thought, could be due to: (1) a twitch in the optic nerve that caused the eyeballs to move, with a resultant movement of the head; (2) a lack of blood in the frontal lobe that caused a momentary dizziness whenever I swung; or (3) the unusual length of my neck. After consultations with an eye specialist, my optic nerves were pronounced first-rate. A brain surgeon assured me my lobes were fine. Dr. Beguine then got down, or rather up, to business. He took 600 X-rays of my neck. After studying them for a week he called me in and said: 'By George, I think I've got it! I believe I've got it!'

"He had me perform my swing while he recorded it on video-tape. Playing it back for me, he said: 'Notice the head movement. It more than moves. It wobbles.'

"And, indeed, he was correct. It was not a movement, but a wobble.

" 'Never had a case like it,' Dr. Beguine said. 'You're double-jointed in the region of the third ancillary neck vertebra!'

"The solution to my problem was both ingenious and simple. Dr. Beguine devised a neck brace that he attached with three straps —one under the crotch and the others under my arms. 'Try swing-ing,' he said.

"I found that it was necessary to stand absolutely straight, stiff-legged, and with no body movement in order to swing a club. I went back to Weinerblut's practice cage, and hit several balls into the target area of the canvas, using only arms and hands. Weiner-blut said not a word. After 20 swings or so, he slid off the stool to the floor.

"The winter's work on my swing did a world of good. My new swing got me off the tee easily a hundred yards and more down the fairway. First time out, I broke 120. I now play regularly at 110. For anyone with the same problem I recommend both Weinerblut and Dr. Beguine, who, by the way, has now patented the neck brace."

"Dr. Beguine devised a neck brace that he attached with three straps . . ."

4 GEOMETRY AND PHYSIOLOGY

THE SWING AND rhythm of the Double Bogey Golfer are to that of a good player what a pneumatic drill is to a Bach fugue. In musical terms, this is the equivalent of what the really good player does:

．　．　．

And this is what the Double Bogey Golfer does:

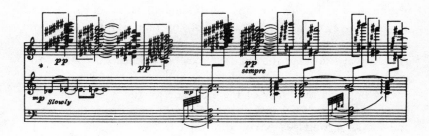

Observe the flowing simplicity of the first example. Observe the economy of means, the grace of the melody, the curve of the phrase, the inevitability of the logic. Everything is in place, everything is smooth and coordinated, moving coherently and directly to a goal.

But observe the second example. It is all disjunct anarchy, everything jumbled together without respect for basic law. The movement is spasmodic, the chords grate on the nerves, the musical flow is definitely of the elbows-flying variety. (It happens to be a section of the *Concord* Sonata by Charles Ives. Ives was not a golfer, as far as we know, and obviously a good thing, too.)

The good golfers swing with left-side control, avoiding right-hand pressure, using a full arc. The Double Bogey Golfer, if he pauses to think at all, has a left hand that does not know what the right hand is doing. That is only just, for the right hand does not know what the left hand is doing. Moreover, the hips of the Double Bogey Golfer are confused about what the legs should be doing. Also there is no relation between lower body and shoulder turn. The Double Bogey Golfer's swing is a mixture of desperation, dissonance, and despair—the three Ds of the Double Bogey Golfer.

Your pro generally tells you that's because you are trying to hit the ball too hard.

Tell him not to be silly.

It is because you are only trying to hit the ball, period.

Here we get into geometrical physiology. It is the order of things that the Double Bogey Golfer is not built as other men. Around

300 B.C., Erasistratus, the father of anatomy, observed that there were nerves of sensation and nerves of motion. It was a true observation, and still holds for most of the human race. But not for the Double Bogey Golfer, who has a hookup that confuses sensation and motion. An order from the brain is sent down to keep the left side forward; instead the left side goes back. Each side of the trochanter moves in a different direction, the tendon of the extensor brevis opposes the inner of the extensor longus pollicis, and the result is a topped shot or a shank, depending upon whether or not the adductor longus is extended or dilated.

That makes life difficult for the Double Bogey Golfer.

The Double Bogey Golfer's swing is a mixture of desperation, dissonance, and despair . . .

If the physiology of the Double Bogey Golfer is a case of bad connections and imperfect synapses, his geometry is even worse. It is definitely non-Euclidean. When the Double Bogey Golfer swings, his club face does not meet the ball on any kind of plane, because with him there are no planes. Or straight lines, for that matter. The jerky, rushed swing of the Double Bogey Golfer is better illustrated by the ups and downs of a fever chart than in terms of a consecutive series of arcs.

Natural laws do not pertain to the Double Bogey Golfer. When he plays a ball in the middle of the fairway with a clear, dead-ahead shot to the green, he lines up with his feet pointing 30 degrees off line, aiming directly at the rough. Yet he *thinks* he is aiming at the flag. When he addresses his 20-foot putt, after examining the green from all angles, after holding his putter twixt thumb and forefinger and authoritatively squinting his eyes at the hole, after lying on his belly to observe the roll of the surface and the depth of the grass and the direction the grass is growing, after testing the strength of the wind and smoothing down the turf— after all this, he carefully places the head of the putter at an angle obtuse to the cup, and swings with the force of a gorilla with a mad on. The long return putt always ends up short. Overcompensation.

It is thus clear that, since natural laws are not his, the Double Bogey Golfer has to evolve his own geometry and physiology. The geometry can be expressed in three axioms:

Axiom I: A 150-yard drive down the middle is better than a 155-yard slice into the rough.

Axiom II: Three straight 150-yard shots equal 450 yards and three strokes.

Axiom III: A 155-yard slice into the rough followed by three shots to get out equal four shots.

Memorize these. They are your Euclid, your Bible. From the three axioms, certain postulates inevitably follow:

Postulate I: Keep out of the rough.

Postulate II: Keep on the fairway.

Or, to put it another way:

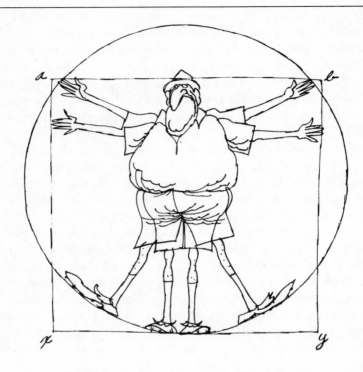

. . . since natural laws are not his, the Double Bogey Golfer has to evolve his own geometry and physiology.

Postulate I: Keep on the fairway.

Postulate II: Keep out of the rough.

Which is followed by another postulate, also basic:

Postulate III: Always swing in the direction of the flag.

To put Postulate III into scientific terms: If you are at point A, aiming at point B, swing toward the direction of B. No matter what you may think, your direction is AB.

Postulate III is not generally known to the Double Bogey Golfer. But it has been proved, and has been known in golfing circles since the days of Homer (who, himself a golfer, in Book VIII of the Odyssey described a fine wedge shot: "Sonorous through the shaded air it sings,/ . . . tempestuous as it flies,/ The crowd gaze upward while it cleaves the skies"), that if the club face is hurtled in the direction of the target, the ball has a better chance of heading in that direction than if the club face is hurtled away from the target.

So much for the geometry of the Double Bogey Golfer. Returning to the physiology, there are only two things to remember. The human body is a cunningly made instrument, in push-pull opposition, with all kinds of complicated physical, chemical, and electronic things going on all at once. Great men of medicine, philosophers, and thinkers in all fields don't begin to understand how it works, so why should you? No; the only two things the Double Bogey Golfer should remember are:

1. Don't try to hit the ball too hard, because you will then (a) slice it, (b) top it, (c) shank it, or (d) miss it.

2. Don't try to hit the ball too easy, because you will then (a) slice it, (b) top it, (c) shank it, or (d) miss it.

5 YOU AND YOUR HEAD

"AND WHAT DID you do wrong?" asks the pro.

"I lifted my head."

"And where should your head be?"

"My head should be down."

Lowering chin toward chest is not a mark of shame or ignominy. Nor is it required only of double bogey players asking indulgence for the inadequacy of their game. It applies equally to all golfers and is the fundamental posture of the sport.

Still, some men simply cannot do it. And there must be a reason why intelligent and sensitive golfers, who have mastered demanding disciplines and complicated crafts, cannot remember to keep their eyes aimed at the ground as their club head travels toward, into, and past their ball.

The failure to keep one's head properly positioned is listed by Dr. Fergus Grievas in *The Young Physician's Guide to Golfing Maladies,* where it is termed "Brindleback's Complaint." The entry is brief and simple. "Brindleback's Complaint is the chronic inability to keep one's head down." The book gives no clue to cause or cure.

Who, you ask, was Brindleback, and what was his complaint? He was no champion. At best, he shot double bogey. But this was in the first part of the 17th century when the Royal and Ancient Club at Saint Andrews was little more than a century old. Brindleback was not a member. He belonged to the Honourable Company of Edinburgh, although he brought no great honour to their colors. This distressed him sorely, for he was a young man who demanded much of himself. Third son of the laird of Glen Divot, he was a champion archer, a superior horseman and swordsman. Only at golf was he constantly bested, and by lads lower born and less skilled in all the other pastimes that filled the days of the sporting gentry.

There came a time when Brindleback could no longer bear the scorn of his fellows and the disappointment in his father's eyes. He took himself north to Frither Glen, home of the renowned Mac-Teague.

For three days, Brindleback waited upon MacTeague, but the sage would not receive him. Impatiently, the highborn lad came early on the fourth morning to pound upon MacTeague's door. When the door stayed shut and barred, he turned on his heels and strode angrily away. He had taken no more than four paces, when a voice rich and booming demanded, "What's yer hurry?"

The words that follow are part of golfdom's richest chronicle. Recorded only in part, they have passed down from one master of Frither Glen to the next and constitute what is called by some "The Way of MacTeague," and by others "The Frither Glen Colloquies."

"What's yer hurry?" asked MacTeague, for it was the man himself, then just past 50, tall and spare with full beard and grizzled whiskers.

"I have no time to waste."

"Then, 'tis just as well ye go," MacTeague agreed, closing the door. But the young man turned back, pleading with such anguish that the great golfer finally relented. "If ye have no time to waste, then ye've no cause to hit at the featherie ball. Golf is a dawdlin', lingerin' game." So MacTeague began and is alleged to have gone on for three hours straight, ruminating on the nature of time in the game of golf. He was perfectly capable of following a train of thought for as many as three days before inquiring just why it was his visitor had come. Eventually, however, Brindleback was allowed to confess his plight.

"I cannot keep my head down."

MacTeague said nothing but handed the youth a length of pine that stood beside the door. "Swing," he commanded.

Brindleback swung, and it was a great, powerful, sweeping swing. His head stayed perfectly still. It failed to come up, for it had never gone down.

"Aye," said MacTeague.

"Just so," said the lad. "The guilty eye the ground, the shameful and the base. The vanquished bow their heads, the vassal and the slave."

"And never the son of the laird of Glen Divot?"

"To no man save the king."

"And to God," roared the old golfer. "Do you not lower your proud head to pray?"

"I do."

"Then pray, you young ass."

"Over a featherie ball?"

"Not over the ball," growled the sage, "but over God's great, round earth. Pray you walk it in peace, feel warmth on the back of your neck and turf underfoot, smell the sea off the links, see the sky, sand, water and grass."

"Are you mocking me?" the young man cried.

"Am I?" demanded MacTeague. "Then ask yourself why God made it so you could not hit the ball save you bow your head. Aye, and what makes the ball to travel true is not just how you hold your head but what you hold inside it. Fill it with selfish thoughts of gain or victory and watch the ball dart straight to the gorse or bound into the sea. Fill it with malice and you'll strike at air. But empty it of all save the beauty of the course, the glory of the morning and the goodness of the earth, and watch your ball fly far and fair."

"Then pray, you young ass."

6 THE SLICE

~~~~~~

"WHY DOES IT always go to the right?"

The question is asked with true pain. Son asks father. Wife asks husband. Golfer asks pro. And the answer is always the same. "Because *you* made it go to the right."

You are *bad*. You are *guilty*. You are *ashamed*, because you made that nice, new ball fly high and wide into the woods, out of bounds or out of play.

"To slice, sir, is no sin." Mark those words. They were said by Herbert de Simplement Woozler to Mungo Park in 1875 (the year Mungo and Willie Park were beaten by Young and Old Tom Morris at North Berwick). Only a beginner, Woozler was already a serious student of the game, and he simply did not accept the conventional wisdom (and the dominant theory today). He knew that it was not *he* who'd made the ball fly right. And so, for the next 27 years, Herbie Woozler concentrated on little else but the origin and nature of the slice, a preoccupation that resulted in a series of business reverses and the eventual bankruptcy of Woozler Woolens late in 1902. But Woozler's financial losses are a small matter, for he discovered the answer and thereby gained immortality.

What Woozler discovered to be true is what every golfer knows in his or her gut. The ball goes to the right because it *wants* to go to the right. That is its nature. The classic banana ball that travels a full 250 yards—175 yards down the fairway and 75 yards to starboard—is the natural path of a drive.

There is nothing abnormal about a slice. It is the way golf balls go. But why do they go that way? For the same reason that water swirls clockwise down drains in the Northern Hemisphere, of course. It would then follow that golf balls below the equator would behave in a contrary manner, slicing left and hooking right. And that is what Woozler discovered. What is more, he eventually determined that the angle of a slice depends almost entirely upon the golfer's latitude. The slice becomes more pronounced the farther one stands from the equator. At either the North or South Pole, a golf ball can be expected to curve a full 90 degrees to the right or left.

Woozler was a long time figuring all this out. Playing in the first round of the Lake Victoria Golf Classic in 1894, he was amazed to find his balls heading straight down the center of the fairway each time he drove. Crediting this consistency to improvements in his own swing, he failed to realize that the location of Lake Victoria, plumb on the equator, might be the real reason. Enlightenment could have come six years earlier had Woozler survived the cut and played for the full four days. But sunspots so altered the gravitational field during the tournament's second day that Woozler's drives would turn right on one hole and left on the next.

It was only in 1900, at the Tierra del Fuego Invitational—just a chip shot from Antarctica—that Woozler realized the truth. Drive after drive disappeared into the scrubby rough left of the fairway. It was the sharp angle of the deviance, almost a full 70 degrees, that caused him to recognize the nature of the phenomenon. Shouting "Eureka," he leaped into the air, grounding his niblick in sand for a two-stroke penalty.

Why has Woozler's wisdom not been shared with the world? Simply because no one took him seriously. When told of Woozler's discovery, the great Harry Vardon sniffed. "Herbie Woozler," he said, dismissing the notion, "that nut with the slice." James Braid was more charitable. He listened. But since he had no trouble with a slice, Woozler's findings failed to interest him.

Like Vardon and Braid, today's pros continue to ignore the evidence that greets their eyes each time a tyro swings a club. The ball goes to the right. "But," say the pros, "if you hit the ball the way *we* hit the ball, then it will not go to the right. Therefore, you must learn to hit the ball as we do." This, understandably, will require many lessons at considerable cost and will result in a handsome profit for the pro and a new swing for you, a swing that will only occasionally allow the ball to follow its natural inclination.

The secret (and every pro knows it) was nearly given away a few years back by an anonymous professional from South Africa, a country located well below the equator. At a golf clinic held in Big Medicine, Montana, the talented foreigner was listening to the plaints of a subdouble bogeyer cursed with a slice that would have made even Woozler weep. Ball after ball flew sharply to the right (Montana, after all, is a good ways north), and when the poor wretch turned and asked, "What can I do for my slice?" the South African forgot himself and replied, "That's no slice, you nit; a slice goes to the *left.*"

The absent-minded South African denies the incident to this day, as do all the professionals present. (The PGA has gone as far as to insist that Big Medicine, Montana, does not exist.) But the duffer involved never forgot that moment. Unfortunately, he has since died, fatally attacked by sand flies in the right bunker off the 16th green of his home course. Nevertheless, the moment at Big Medicine is not lost, for it forms the major part of the late slicer's contribution to the Oral History of Golf Project at Montana Mountain State College.

The answer to the slice, Woozler determined, is not to be found in the swing but in the golf course. The course should obviously be designed to follow the natural flight of the golf ball. Woozler conceived such a course, but the frustration and cost he encountered while building the never-completed Swirling Dervish Links, outside of Glasgow, broke his heart and put Woozler Woolens into receivership.

As conceived by Woozler, the course would consist of a series of ever-contracting concentric circles, with the 18th green at the very center. Each hole bends to the right, and the degree of right-hand turn becomes more pronounced as one rounds the course. The opening holes (the only ones actually constructed) incline only gently to the right, and a full five of them are required to complete the outermost ring. There are four holes in the next ring, three holes in the third and two each in the fourth and fifth (these spiral upward). By the 18th, the right-hand angle has become so extreme that the final hole consists of two complete loops in 417 yards, culminating in a well-trapped green atop the hillock known as Woozler Heights.

Although the golfing fraternity has never recognized the value of Woozler's work, the military was quick to see that Herbie was on to a good thing. Indeed, it was partly to study the "Woozler effect" that the Royal Navy prevailed upon the Royal Geographic Society to sponsor Captain Scott's first expedition to Antarctica. The golfing experiments conducted during this venture were classified "Eyes Only" and thus were never mentioned in Scott's book, *The Voyage of the "Discovery."* Nevertheless, the prodigious strength of the Woozler effect in the Ross Sea area caused the Royal Navy to produce 100 gross of high explosive golf balls and 40 sets of matched drivers for issue to the Arctic Squadron.

"The Woozler weapon," wrote the Secretary of the Admiralty Board, "will enable the Royal Navy to shoot around corners." Just why a naval vessel might need such a capacity was never explained, and the experiment came to a tragic end in 1911, when the H.M.S. *Treacle* was lost at sea during a practice driving session off Greenland. According to survivors, one of the ship's company duck-hooked a high explosive ball into the ammunition locker, causing it to blow up and the ship subsequently to sink. Undoubtedly, this is the most severe penalty ever taken for an out-of-bounds shot.

Although the British abandoned their interest in the Woozler effect, the United States launched a major study of it soon after entering World War II. The Staten Island Project, as it was called, was initially considered just as promising as the more celebrated Manhattan Project, although its results were somewhat less dramatic. Nor were the Germans far behind. Their experimental station on the Dortmund Driving Range (part of Operation *Rechtgeflugen)* was given the same high priority for Allied bombers as the missile center at Peenemünde.

Lest you imagine that interest in the Woozler effect has flagged, ask yourself why, at great cost and with considerable difficulty, NASA transported a six iron and golf ball to the moon. Although only one shot was played on television, informed sources insist that a long series of "moon shots" were part of the experiment that verified the Woozler effect on earth's lone satellite.

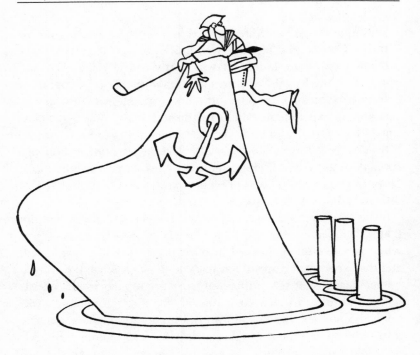

... the H.M.S. Treacle was lost at sea during a practice driving session ...

Fascinating, you say. But the question remains. How does the Double Bogey Golfer minimize the effects of the Woozler phenomenon on his own game? In other words, how does one restrain the ball from following its inclination to go right?

There are many answers—keep your head down, follow through, hit from inside out, pivot on your backswing, close your stance, open your stance, close your eyes, breathe deeply, don't breathe. And *one* other. To keep the ball from going to the right, *hit it to the right.*

Yes indeed, to keep the ball from going right, hit it right.

Ask your pro. He will confirm it. As the pros tell it, the golf ball travels right when hit left because the club head is drawn across it imparting right-hand spin to the missile and sending it curving off toward disaster.

This is nonsense, if one considers the golf ball's point of view. Understand that the simple spheroid has a natural urge to move to the right. Hit toward the center of the fairway, the ball will follow its own inclination and move rightward in what golfers describe as a fade. The ball is shocked by the blow. Anxious only to escape further agony and humiliation, it moves forward rapidly from the source of its distress. When the ball is struck from the right rear by a club that follows it swiftly from right to left, then it takes action to avoid continuing on this shameful and painful course. It veers *sharply* to the right.

To correct the slice, the blow must come from the left rear and the club pursue the ball on its initial rightward flight. To avoid further punishment or embarrassment, the ball will turn to the left and, freed from the Woozler effect, proceed in the direction most appropriate to the play of the hole.

It should be noted that the findings of Woozler were not recognized until recently in most Communist countries, where credit for a similar discovery was given to the Romanian golf theorist Sandor Popic. The 1984 edition of *How the Party Stands on Sports,* issued by the Bulgarian State Publishing Council, contains an article titled "Dialectics of the Slice." According to the authors, Yetta Smetna and Basil Bulba, "The golf ball must be perceived as a political body, for it follows similar rules of behavior. Pushed radically to the left, the ball reacts by moving to the right. Forced to the right, it responds by turning to the left. When no limitations are placed upon its flight, the ball reveals a marked tendency to drift rightward, and the concerned socialist sportsman must remain always vigilant to prevent this reactionary development."

7 THROUGH HAZARDS AND ROUGH

~~~~~~

"Is IT . . . is it . . . there?"

Yes, it is there, in the rough, where, according to Medford Redford's *Never Touch the Fairway,* the Double Bogey Golfer will place his drive 31 percent of the time. (Because Redford's figures reflect only those drives actually played out and do not account for mulligans and out-of-bounds shots, a more likely percentage would be closer to 45.)

Most Double Bogey Golfers fear the rough. But then, most of them also fear bunkers, water hazards, downhill lies, divots, clover, and mole holes. Some even tremble before perfectly scrumptious lies that leave their ball seated atop a soft tuft of grass on a broad plateau. "It is the fear in our hearts and not the failing of our limbs that make us what we are," Thorvald MacDougal once said, and MacDougal was the greatest golfer who never broke 90.

Playing out of the rough or from a hazard is to be rightly feared. It is supposed to be difficult. But is it really? Not the way it was when MacDougal strode the links, in the days of wooden shafts and iron men. The Scots are not a wasteful people and it was never their intent to play golf upon land that might be used for some other and more practical purpose, like growing oats or grazing sheep. It was the marshy, sandy, windy, worthless real estate beside the sea that they chose, the links-land. Along these strands, the game evolved. And the skilled golfsman was not one who merely kept his ball straight and hit it long. He was the one best able to hit and hold to the smallish clumps of grass that appeared infrequently in this hostile terrain. At that time, difficulty and not simple distance was the measure of a golf course.

Not so today, no matter what the USGA alleges or the PGA proclaims. The touring pros and low-handicap amateurs have demanded courses suited to their talents—long, broad avenues of fairway as regular as Astroturf, with wide borders of demirough so closely trimmed that a sheep would starve in it. For hazards, there is an occasional tree (well pruned) and bunkers flat as a flapper's bosom.

Golfers today are bred and trained, like popular breeds of dogs, to exaggerate one specific characteristic. Just as Yorkies must be small, sheepdogs large, collies have thin heads, bassets drag their bellies, today's golfer must have a bestial drive. Only thus can he par the well-manicured holes of absurd length and basic simplicity that now prevail. But golf, as it was meant to be played, is not the repetitive routine of a giant drive followed by a wedge to the green and one or two putts. It is a mad scramble across the links, an adventure fraught with constant peril where fortune changes shot by shot. And that kind of golf is played today only by Double Bogey Golfers.

To be fair, the touring pros face a rugged layout or two. Courses are allowed to get shaggy for tournament play and pins are placed in awkward spots. But the average club spread is nothing that Allan Robertson, the great champion of Saint Andrews, would recognize as a golf course. This, to be sure, is the work of near-scratch members more willing to smooth out the rough spots on the course than in their game. But it is done with the foolish acquiescence of the bogey and double-bogey membership. Foolish, we say, because the rough is the Double Bogey Golfer's best friend.

Nowhere are men of different handicaps more equal than amidst the brambles and the thickets. "Gorse," as the illustrious Mac-Teague has said, "is golf's great leveler."

A 2-handicapper is no more able to put his ball through a tree than is a 36-handicapper. Each must take the same stroke when all that's needed is a two-foot bobble to place the ball back in line with the green. A truly unplayable lie is equally unplayable for all golfers. What is more, when high handicap meets low handicap on a treacherous and hazard-ridden hole, where misfortune is indiscriminately strewn, the high handicapper will fare relatively better.

Take an average four-par hole that the scratch player finishes in par and the Double Bogey Golfer plays in six. On this hole, the double bogeyer has taken two more shots than his opponent's four, a difference of 50 percent. And why has he taken these extra strokes? Because he has gotten into trouble. Even on this simple-minded belter's delight (400 straight yards from the tee, with traps politely flanking a broad and deep green) he has found the bad places. But suppose we ruck up this hole, narrow the fairway, stick a thicket 250 yards out in the center, run traps across the front of the now shallow green. The odds are that the scratch player will get into trouble. So, you say, will the Double Bogey Golfer. Quite true, but the difference is that he was already in trouble before the hole was altered.

The way the hole was initially played, the Double Bogey Golfer sliced his drive into the rough some 175 yards from the tee. He hit out only well enough to lie about 90 yards off the green. Next, he pulled his nine-iron shot into the left-hand bunker, blasted clear but far enough from the pin so that two putts were needed to hole out. A perfect six. The scratch player belted some 240 yards, then hit a six-iron down the fairway and the ball bounded and ran up past the pin. He also took two putts. A garden-variety four.

Replaying the hole once the improvements have been made, the scratch player puts his drive into the mid-fairway thicket and needs one shot to get clear. His iron to the green cannot hit in front (that's where we've put the new bunker). He must play a longer club, and his ball now runs off the back of the shallower green into the heavy rough we've just planted there. It is one up and two down for a total of six.

But what happens to the Double Bogey Golfer? He was in the rough first time around, and he is there again. His second and third shots are no better than before. Only now his blast from the bunker runs off the green but not as far off as his opponent's longer, stronger, and flatter shot. Since the high-handicap man chips no better than he blasts, he is still two putts away from the pin when he gains the green.

Now, look at the score. The regular scratch player has taken a six, while the Double Bogey Golfer ends up with a seven. The one-stroke difference between their two scores represents a variance, not of 50 percent, but of only 16 percent. If we assume that every hole on the course could be similarly reconstructed, then the Double Bogey Golfer, who usually shoots about 108, would end up with 126. But his adversary's anticipated 72 would blossom to 108 (double bogey, by God).

The lesson is obvious. The rough is your friend. Learn to love it, for it will snatch your opponent's balls and make him cry for mercy. Why do Double Bogey Golfers join the chorus crying for flatter fairways and more docile rough, fewer hazards, and shallower traps when such design is plainly against their best interests? No matter how the course is designed or tended, *they* are going to get into trouble anyway.

What the Double Bogey Golfer must do, *tomorrow,* is to walk his course with an eye for the site of future snares and snaggles, creepers and tangles, and ball-grabbing scruff. There are limits to the ways in which one may legitimately rough up a golf course, but it might pay to lay hands on Telemachus Pettigrew's *The Hundred Most Horrible Hazards.*

It was Pettigrew who recorded such notable hazards as the bunker of shaved ice added to the Aklavik Municipal Links, site of Canada's Northwest Territorial Championship. Because the temperature was about 30 below during all of the three-day event, the ice had to be reshaved for every mittened foursome.

A more satisfactory bunker was created for the Battle Creek Open. It consisted of a large hole, filled with Rice Krispies. Those who shot out of it during practice rounds said the cereal took a wedge easily, but they complained that the footing was difficult and the noise—the continuous crunching sound, not to mention an occasional pop, snap, or crackle—unbearable. At any rate, a sufficient number of faint hearts protested, and the bunker was refilled with more conventional materials before the first round began.

Out in Omaha, however, at the Deep Dish Country Club, a tournament for the Mountain States Food Processors Convention featured four bunkers about the 18th green, each filled with a different flavor gelatin mold. The traps were deemed playable, although the wisdom of this decision soon became questionable as one contestant after another ventured into the ooze, flailing and scooping frantically at balls that sank slowly from view. As the day wore on and the temperature rose, the gelatin molds softened and were filled with foot pits (impossible to rake).

Only one player whose ball entered any of the molds was able to complete the hole. At 3:27 p.m., when the gelatin had sunk seven feet below the lip, Stanford S. Brickle of West Orange, New Jersey, entered the front right-hand bunker (lime flavored) wearing waders and carrying a vintage water-iron. This hickory-shafted antique featured a uniquely open face—the center of the club head had been cut away to reduce drag as it was swept through the water.

Striking swiftly, as his ball reached the first fathom mark, Brickle sent it onto the green, while he himself sank beneath the gooey tide. When Brickle's ball reached the green, along with two quarts of gelatin and 14 cherries (one of which holed out), the player was being hauled from the bunker where his waders remained permanently embedded. Shaky but game, Brickle staggered to the green only to require 17 putts to move his sticky ball into the cup.

Less famous than the gelatin traps at Deep Dish is an incident from the final round of the club championship at Hemlock Cups, near Moline, Illinois, in the autumn of 1978. With defending champion Quint Derwint up one, challenger Sal Slagle teed off on the

A more satisfactory bunker was created . . . filled with Rice Krispies.

17th and sliced out of bounds, into the four-lane highway alongside the hole. Then, Derwint hooked his own drive sharply. The speeding missile struck a telephone pole and bounded even farther left into a thick woods that separated the fairway from the practice range.

As Slagle hit his second drive, Derwint's caddie dashed for the spot where the champion's ball seemed to have been heading. A sharp-eyed and plucky lad, he braved brambles and poison sumac to venture where few members had trod. His goal turned out to be an open space along a dry creek bed. There, in a sizable declivity, were several hundred golf balls. Over the years, misdirected practice shots had found their way off the range by means of the creek bed. Somewhere among them, the caddie was convinced, lay Derwint's Club Special.

When Derwint, Slagle, and the crowd that had been following the play arrived on the scene, a series of questionable rulings was made by the referee, Homer Bigheart, a local attorney then representing Derwint's wife in a divorce action.

First, Quint claimed the ball-filled pit was an artificial obstruction. Bigheart said, "No." The balls in the hole, he maintained, were not purposely placed there. Instead, they had arrived in a most natural manner.

Next, Quint insisted he had an unplayable ball. Bigheart ruled that he could only move it to another position within the pit.

Finally, it dawned upon Derwint that if he failed to locate his ball among the several hundred on the scene, within the allotted five minutes, he could legitimately claim a lost ball, leaving him no worse off than his out-of-bounds opponent. But just as he'd finished puzzling the idea through, his eager-beaver caddie sang out, "There it is, Mr. Derwint!"

"Where?"

"There," the boy repeated, pointing at the near side of the pit, where Quint was just able to make out his identification mark on a ball lying flush with the others in that section.

Bigheart declared the adjacent balls could not be moved, rejecting Quint's contention that they were the equivalent of dry twigs or leaves. "*Nothing* can be moved," said Bigheart. "You're in a hazard." Then the referee leveled a one-stroke penalty against the champion for moving his ball when it shifted with others in the pit as Derwint strode among them. Fearful of incurring more penalties, Quint swung quickly, using an open-faced seven iron. At least six balls left the pit, traveling distances that ranged from 40 to 120 yards. None of them was Derwint's.

At this point, the champion was lying three by his own count and the crowd's. "Eight," said Bigheart, charging him one stroke for each of the six balls he had struck.

"There's no penalty for hitting a ball that's not yours, when you are in the rough," Derwint argued.

"It wasn't a case of mistaken identity," Bigheart replied. "Your ball was right there. You missed it, and you hit six range balls instead. They count as practice strokes." Saying that, he changed his ruling and charged Derwint an extra stroke for having missed his own ball. "You're playing 10."

Derwint was unable to locate his own ball among those left in the pit. Finally, he took another penalty stroke—for a lost ball—and returned to the tee to drive again, playing 11. Understandably rattled, Quint not only lost the 17th but the 18th as well—and the championship. But he did not lose his wife. So horrified was this lady by her lawyer's harsh rulings that she began to question his actions on her behalf. She thought short and hard about the divorce and their marriage. She took a long look at her estranged mate, noble in adversity (he'd been unbearable in triumph), and charged through the crowd on the 18th green to throw herself into his arms.

Clutched to Derwint's chest, Anne (for that was the lady's name) heard him mumbling softly under his breath. She snuggled closer. "Should have played an eight iron," he was saying.

Although Derwint's fall was caused by the misfortune of finding his ball, most players are undone by losing one. Finding the ball is perhaps the least recognized of basic golfing skills. For Double Bogey Golfers the easiest way is to get hold of a good caddie. On courses where caddies are still available, it always seems that the best of them end up carrying for the best golfers. This makes sense only from the caddie's point of view. He can learn more from a low-handicap player than from a high-handicap one. Besides, the work is easier and more agreeable. But caddies should be assigned on the basis of need, and the Double Bogey Golfer's need is greatest. He requires more advice, comfort, and aid in the location of misdirected shots than any others among the membership.

The traditional method for the unassisted golfer to find a lost ball is to line himself up with a prominent object along the line of flight and keep marching toward that landmark until the ball appears underfoot. This is most useful when the ball leaves the tee or fairway on a straight line. When it departs thence on an angle or following a path of several angles or traveling in an arc, it is considerably more difficult.

Some golfers, to be sure, can never line up their shot more specifically than with "those woods out there on the right." They can always palm an extra ball as they enter the rough, slip it through the waistband of their trousers and let it trickle down their leg onto the ground (where some other member of the foursome will find it). But if they shrink from such deception, burdened both by a faulty sense of direction and an active conscience, they may try the system MacTeague of Frither Glen taught his disciples: "Free the mind's eye to see the hidden ball."

First, you must clear your mind of extraneous thoughts, including score, number of strokes, amount wagered, day of week, number of children, name of wife, and the like. Then, facing in the general direction taken by the ball, try to recapture the sight of the ball in the sky. Next, try to see the entire hole as it would appear to the ball and ask yourself: "Traveling at this speed and in this direction, where do I land?"

Just pose the question; do not force the answer.

Wait, mind open and receiving on all channels. It will come to you. You will see a vast stretch of woodland, then a specific area, next a patch, and finally a spot where the ball is sure to be found.

When you reach that spot, do not dash about punishing the shrubbery with a club. Stand silently in the center of the patch. Let your mind run free and remember that the ball does not wish to be found. It will head for the nearest cover and snuggle down out of sight. So proceed to the nearest cover. If the ball is not there, then you are obviously too preoccupied with worldly affairs to use the MacTeague technique and you are best off getting a good caddie, a long-suffering partner, or a lot of golf balls.

But let us suppose that you have found the ball. What then? MacDougal's advice to the minimally skilled golfer is just as valid today as it was more than 100 years ago:

> *When in brier, gorse and such,*
> *Never try to do too much;*
> *Forget your mashie's mighty clout,*
> *And concentrate on getting out.*

It is not given to the Double Bogey Golfer to go boldly for the green. He must rather go timidly toward the fairway—but not too timidly. Studying and planning an awkward shot from a difficult lie is of little use to a high handicapper. The more he meditates, the more difficult the shot appears. So, strike quickly and for the nearest clearing (on whatever fairway is most handy). It is best to use shorter clubs because their heads are bigger and more likely to make contact with the ball.

Keep the club head open.

Higher numbered woods are also useful implements in the rough because they come more forcefully through the greenery than do irons. When balls are teed atop clumps of rough-weed, then lower numbered woods (even the mighty driver) may be tried.

A final word about water hazards: *NO*. Don't go near the water. Take your penalty and try again. The less than special golfer who ignores this dictum will add mightily to his score and place himself

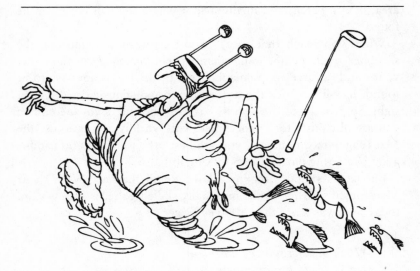

Golfers have drowned, been brutally nibbled by irate fish . . .

in other peril. Golfers have drowned, been brutally nibbled by irate fish, and contracted chronic catarrh, all while splashing about after a sunken ball to avoid a one-stroke penalty.

8   SAND

SAND. IT IS neutral, generally inoffensive stuff. Certainly nobody should be scared by sand. What is it, after all, except pulverized rock or minerals, mostly quartz, with smaller amounts of feldspar, garnet, tourmaline, zircon, rutile, anatase, topaz, staurolite, cyanite, andalusite, chlorite, biotite, hornblende, augite, chert, and iron oxides, with traces of olivine, enstatite, tremolite, chromite, and the debris of calcareous shells?

To know is to understand.

Yet there is no more terrible moment in life than when you have to descend into a stupid bunker to hit a stupid ball onto a stupid green with a stupid sand wedge. Even good golfers have been known to stand in sand, breathing heavily, quaking for a sizable segment of eternity, before summoning up the courage to make a pitiful jab at the ball. If the good golfer is so affected, consider the paralytic collapse of the Double Bogey Golfer, who knows—*knows*

—that he is only going to dig the ball in deeper when he offers at it.

He has a legitimate grievance. He spends more time in sand than a worm does in dirt, and the more time he spends, the worse he gets. Failure begets failure. He knows he is not going to explode out in less than three. He also knows that when he finally does, the ball is going to rise majestically and descend into the opposite trap. Furthermore, he knows that if he tries to pick the ball out with a pitching wedge or a nine iron, he is going to get a longer drive than he ever did off the tee. No wonder he stands there, arms trembling, thrusting rashly at the ball, trying to lift it, trying to *order* it to the green by psychokinetic power.

So it goes, as Kurt Vonnegut says. Death is in the air.

There is a solution, and perhaps its very simplicity has kept it from being recognized. The solution, baldly stated, is to avoid bunkers. It stands to reason that if you are not in one, you don't have to hit out of one. The golfer in general, and the Double Bogey Golfer in particular, must be prepared to do *anything* to avoid bunkers.

It has been said that brave men are all the braver because they know what fear is. Nobody will blame a man for retreating in the face of suicidal odds. There is a time to be brave and a time to be prudent (even cowardly, if necessary), and the time for prudence comes when you are faced with a pitch over a bunker. If you go for the green you will inevitably land in the trap, thus ending up with 118 or 120 rather than your usual 110. Prudence therefore dictates that you *must* play the ball sideways or even, in extreme cases, backward. Anything for a clear shot at the green. One often must retreat in order to attack, as Clausewitz or Napoleon pointed out.

And as Arnold Schoenberg well realized.

The great Austrian composer, who worked out the 12-tone musical system around 1923, used his own musical theories while playing golf. In Schoenberg's dodecaphonic system, the 12 notes of the scale are carefully arranged into a series in which no single note is repeated. That "series," or "row," forms the basis of the entire composition. The row is subject to manipulation. It can be played upside down (inverted), backward (retrograde), or backward and upside down (retrograde inversion).

During the years that Schoenberg and Stravinsky were living in Los Angeles, they once had a golf match. Both were out for blood; they really did not like each other very much. Along about the fourth hole they both found themselves faced with nemesis—a pitch over the bunker. Stravinsky's pitch landed on the beach. He let out a cry more grating than anything to be found in his *Sacre du Printemps*. But Schoenberg? Schoenberg took out a seven iron, faced backward, and sent the ball 10 yards or so at an angle that would present a direct shot to the green.

"Retrograde motion," he chuckled.

Then, using the same club, he rolled up to easy putting distance. Stravinsky, a sore loser, claimed that the shot was illegal. Schoenberg hauled out the rule book and defied Stravinsky to point out anything that prevented retrograde motion on the golf course. It may be more than coincidence that, only a few years later, Stravinsky was composing music based on the Schoenberg system.

Admittedly it takes a man of great inner strength to hit *away* from a bunker. Most golfers simply refuse to do it, much as it makes sense and lowers the score. They are creatures of convention, alarmed at anything that departs from routine, and they refuse to hit sideways or backward. They are afraid of being called chicken, or worse. Lemminglike, they swarm to their doom, taking insane chances, all of which result in popping or rolling into bunkers.

Under these circumstances, therefore, it is worthwhile to have a better knowledge of the enemy—sand itself. As pointed out above, sand is pulverized rock or minerals, mostly quartz, with smaller amounts of feldspar, garnet, tourmaline, zircon, rutile, anatase, topaz, staurolite, cyanite, andalusite, chlorite, biotite, hornblende, augite, chert, and iron oxides, with traces of olivine, enstatite, tremolite, chromite, and the debris of calcareous shells.

This is not random encyclopedic information. It is terribly important, for each component of sand obviously has its own specific

Lemminglike, they swarm to their doom . . .

gravity and its own characteristics in relation to the force applied by the striking object—the sand wedge in this case. Clearly, it makes a great deal of difference if you are hitting out of a mixture of felsite, andalusite, and the debris of calcareous shells on the one hand, or a mixture of quartz and anatase on the other. Perhaps the difference is not so pronounced to scratch players, notably insensitive types, but duffers are as delicately tuned as rabbits out for the evening feed. Everything and anything can disturb the Double Bogey Golfer.

So he must learn his sands. A good course is given at the University of Saint Nepomuk in Outer Silesia. There one learns to differentiate between chlorite and hornblende, between topaz and staurolite, and how to use diffraction equipment and a chemical kit. Later, with experience, the quality of the sand can be determined by feel and taste.

There are charts that break down the various components of sand. Never be without one. Otherwise you will have no means of calibrating the correct swing in relation to the sand on your own course.

For instance, it has been demonstrated that a golf ball sneering from sand composed of 60 percent quartz, 22 percent biotite, 14 percent anatase, and 4 percent iron oxides should be sent on its way by hitting *exactly* 2.73146 inches behind it (the specifications are critical; learn to meet them exactly if the chart is to do you any good). With a sand composed of 87 percent chromite, 12 percent tourmaline, and 1 percent chert, it is necessary to hit *exactly* 3.1417 inches behind the ball.

Admittedly this takes a little practice.

In the meantime, Double Bogey Golfers in sand throughout the world had best set their feet firmly, swing through about two inches behind the ball (but really swing through, all the way through), keep the head down, and hope for the best. For the Double Bogey Golfer there are sure ways into a bunker, but no way out. So remember the great truth: If you are not in one, you don't have to hit out of one.

9 EQUIPMENT FOR THE DOUBLE BOGEY GOLFER

NATURALLY HE WANTS the best equipment. Money is no object. For an instrument that will take two or three strokes off his game, that will bring him closer to the magic number of 99, the Double Bogey Golfer will sell house and car, make a pact with Mephistopheles, and backstroke to the Fiji Islands.

But selecting the proper equipment is not easy. Everybody wants a ball that will fly straight and true, that will give an additional five or six feet on the drive, that will land on the green with plenty of backspin. And everybody wants clubs that will provide the impetus for the ball to fly straight and true, to give the backspin, and to do other tricks. The Double Bogey Golfer is more alert to these needs than other more favored species, for he needs more help than they do. He therefore makes his purchases very carefully. He studies the technical specifications in the advertisements of his favorite publications, and he may even make a trip or two to the various factories to see for himself and check up on the claims.

He ends up confused—and small wonder.

Should his golf ball be the Dunlop Maxfli Tournament HT, with its balata cover and its unique clustered dimple pattern? Or the Ram Tour Lithium Balata? If the latter is chosen, he should know that the Ram Tour Lithium Balata is not a true balata ball, but has a cover of lithium combined with various synthetics equivalent to the true balata from the South American palanquin tree. (Statistics courtesy of the Ram Golf Corporation, which makes the claim that, because of its Diacrylate core, its ball will travel seven to 10 yards longer than a ball without that remarkable core.)

But wait a minute, Spalding and its Top-Flite are not about to be undone from their market share. Top-Flite used to be just a Top-Flite. But when other balls began encroaching on its popularity, Spalding met the competition by coming up with Top-Flite XL, with its dimple pattern claimed to send the ball higher as well as farther in its trajectory; this was followed by the Top-Flite II and then Top-Flite XLII, which (again according to company statistics) has an improved super center and a radiused icosahedral dimple design! However, the Spalding issue is confused, if not compromised, by the same company's Tour Edition, which has a Zinthane cover and is supposed to fly the longest of all, making it even longer than its Top-Flite "longest ball." And are there even more super designs in our future?

Acushnet's wound and balata-covered Titleist is an old and honored standby on the tour, but a good many Double Bogey Golfers have avoided it because of its tendency to cut when the swing is not all it should be and the ball is contacted strangely. Quickly the company came out with a solid core, surlyn-covered ball, the Pinnacle. But good was not good enough, so Titleist followed a trend with the lithium-blend-covered Pinnacle Gold, which presumably made the nonmetallic Pinnacle obsolete.

This barely covers the wide range of balls available to the Double Bogey Golfer, who is forced to face a question of great import, and with no easy answer. How is he to determine the accuracy of the many claims of great distance, accurate flight, and feather-soft landings on the green?

To confound the confusion, even such intellects as Nobel prize physicists would find it hard to understand the way golf balls are tested. What is he to think when a company claims its ball will go such a number of yards farther than any other ball, and six other companies guarantee the same thing? Is somebody, uh, by any chance, *lying?* One USGA tester inadvertently mentioned to an inquiring reporter that he knew of a ball that *did* go farther than any other ball, but he resolutely refused to identify it. He is reported to have received hundreds of pleas (along with bribe offers and even threats) from Double Bogey Golfers to reveal its brand name. As of this writing it must be known as the unnamed ball that cannot be named. (We continue to investigate, however.)

Yet the search for the perfect golf ball is nothing compared to the search for perfect woods and irons. The Double Bogey Golfer reads the conflicting claims of the golf club manufacturers and ends up able to do nothing. He is in the position of a sex fiend in a harem. There are so many choices that indecision prevails.

It is not that the manufacturers make exaggerated claims, or anything like that. Everybody knows how honest and, indeed, modest they are. They want to help you; they are in business only to serve you and make you happy. Yet for some reason each golf club manufacturer is convinced that he and he alone has the secret. This he believes from the very bottom of his corporate heart.

The Double Bogey Golfer still remains confused. Should he favor Wilson's Laser X2 Steelwood with its parabolic head shape and optimal face angle? Should he throw his custom to True Temper's Gold Plus R400, which boasts a frequency-matched Gold Plus shaft? But did you know that the New Maxfli Tour Limited clubs helped some pictured but unnamed nice-looking guy in its ad to "shave 7 strokes off my game"? Something definitely to consider there, if the fellow can be believed. Seven strokes? Every round?!

The Japanese, as you undoubtedly know, have entered the golf club field as they have entered just about every other where a dollar or two can be made. Double Bogey Golfers must stay alert. Look what the Japanese have done with computers, video recorders, automobiles, and cameras. Think of Sony, Nikon, and Honda. Are these not names that speak of great technical prowess? Perhaps, too, with golf clubs, although Toyotas are not yet on the scene.

However, Izuno offers (at a price, admittedly) its MGC ± 35 irons with oversized titanium club heads that provide a 28 percent tighter dispersion range and that will send the ball 14 yards farther, using a five iron.

Karsten of Ping prefers beryllium copper over titanium. His Beryllium Copper Eye2 irons are combined with advanced perimeter weighting and a new cavity shape and weight distribution, and ZZ-Lite Microtaper shafts. Ping has even made a beryllium copper putter. On the other hand, Slotline has thrown down the gauntlet to Ping. Its Inertial Putters are claimed to make you putt 2.5 times better than with the putter you play with now, whatever that might be. A nice touch here is that the Slotline putter comes with a specially made and fitted leather head cover.

There are graphite and boron to contend with. Daiwa and Aldila feature graphite shafts. Daiwa is proud of its Amorphous TRX-T graphite shafts for its metal woods, while Aldila prefers a low torque graphite with boron reinforcement. Don't expect to find these clubs on bargain counters. This is high-tech at its techiest.

The advances are simply mind-boggling, and they come piling at us with each new season. There are now long-shafted putters for those of us who don't like to bend or squat, and gold-shafted metal woods, and oversized putting grips, and forged cavity-backed irons, and we won't even go into the fuss over square or rounded grooves. . . .

Too bad that all of these wonderful tools can't be used at once. But the rules specify that only 14 clubs can be in one bag.

Faced with this plethora of goodness, what can one do but turn to the experts. So venerable Jack Nicklaus is consulted, large as life on videotape. Expertise can go no higher. Watching, listening, reading Nicklaus, taking voluminous notes, one learns to worry about that worrisome thing, the thickness of the grip.

Bet you didn't know *that*.

Seems that Nicklaus is responsive to differences as little as one-sixteenth of an inch in the thickness of a grip. His intelligent fingers prefer grips one-sixteenth of an inch thicker than standard. They also prefer leather grips to rubber or synthetic ones.

Grips that are thicker than standard promote fading or slicing,

Nicklaus warns; thinner than standard grips promote hooking or drawing. The matter, Nicklaus soberly says, "may be worth some experimentation on your part."

Then comes the club itself. The Double Bogey Golfer is faced with a choice of stiff shafts versus a variety of flexible shafts. On this point there is an infinity of options. Basically there are A shafts (whippy), S (stiff), X (extra-stiff), and XX (extra-extra-stiff).

All of these clubs are swing-weighted. Nicklaus, for instance, favors clubs swing-weighted at about D5 to D6. The higher the swing-weight designation, the heavier the club head will feel in relation to the grip end of the club.

Even the great Jack Nicklaus became confused in his experimentation. There was the time he reduced the swing weight of his driver to D1. "To do so without changing shafts I had, of course"—of course—"to reduce the club's head weight, and for a while this posed problems, in that—at least until I got tired—I would swing too fast. Gradually, however, I was able to cure this by developing a driver weighing 13.9 ounces, containing an S shaft and still swing-weighting at D1. . . ."

Wise words from a wise man. But what works for Jack Nicklaus does not always work for the Double Bogey Golfer.

In an effort to resolve the problem, the Bureau of Testing and Statistics (Weights and Measures Division) of the Propulsion Laboratory of the National Drygoods Division, aided by a grant from the Double Bogey Golfers' Association in connection with the ILGWU, recently held a definitive series of tests.

Every club on the market was tried out by a carefully selected panel, no member of which had ever broken 100. In addition, grips of various thicknesses, starting at gradations of .001 millimicron, in all materials from leather to chef foil, were part of the test.

The results conclusively and scientifically proved the following: It makes no difference at all what make of club the Double Bogey Golfer uses. Or what ball he uses.

In the driving test, all of the golfers sampled sliced 132.7 yards, give or take a couple of inches, no matter what club was used. It made no difference whether they were using a 13.9-ounce driver with an S shaft swing-weighted at D2, or a 2.6-ounce club with an A shaft swing-weighted at D24. Similarly, iron shots with any iron, whether tungsten inserted, or Dy-Nertial, or honeycombed with an aerodynamically designed tunnel sole, resulted in a sculled grounder 32.3 yards (again give or take a couple of inches). As for the choice of ball, it was scientifically demonstrated that the compression, whether 75 or 120, made no difference at all.

Thus it scientifically follows that the Double Bogey Golfer can use any club, secure in the knowledge that the results are always going to be the same. Choose your clubs the way you are supposed to choose a puppy from a newly born litter. Shut your eyes, reach down, and grab.

It makes no difference at all what make of club the Double Bogey Golfer uses.

One curious piece of scientifically proved data came out of the tests. Golf gloves naturally were part of the testing, and the overwhelming consensus was that a glove made from the pelts of unborn duckbilled platypuses was the most comfortable and efficient by far. There seemed to be only two slight liabilities: The gloves were available on import only from a small firm in Jiggalong, Australia, and the price was not to be believed. It was also noted that the gloves tended to come apart after every third or fourth hole. The scientifically determined conclusion was that the dedicated Double Bogey Golfer should, under these circumstances, carry a half dozen or so such gloves in his bag.

10 CLUB SELECTION— AND REJECTION

~~~~~~

CHOOSING THE RIGHT club to use for a particular shot is more complex for the Double Bogey Golfer than for the par player. Long and accurate hitters, after considering the condition of the course and such acts of God as wind, rain, and sleet, have only to consult this simple guide found in almost any primer on the game:

CLUB	DISTANCE
Driver	240 yards and up
2 Wood	220 to 265
3 Wood	200 to 250
4 Wood	200 to 225
1 Iron	180 to 215
2 Iron	175 to 205
3 Iron	165 to 200
4 Iron	155 to 190

5 Iron	145 to 180
6 Iron	135 to 170
7 Iron	125 to 160
8 Iron	115 to 150
9 Iron	105 to 140
Pitching Wedge	Edge of green to 100
Sand Wedge	Edge of green to 40

As can be seen, the list makes allowances in lengths obtainable by golfers of varying weight, height, and strength. It does not, however, cater to the Double Bogey Golfer, and for him the guide is all but useless. True enough, there are Double Bogey Golfers who can on occasion hit a driver the requisite 240 yards or more, but the ball, once hit, is seldom found. Obviously, he stops using that club.

The list poses another dilemma in that it contains 15 clubs. The rules allow only 14. With the addition of a putter, two of the listed clubs must be discarded. Furthermore, these days the two wood has all but disappeared from matched sets. Meanwhile the popularity of the five wood has risen, and six and seven woods are seen in many bags. Eight and nine woods have been spotted, particularly on the courses around Myrtle Beach, South Carolina, and there are reports that 15 and 20 woods are being manufactured for the new millionaire classes in Taiwan and South Korea.

So, complications abound for the Double Bogey Golfer about to buy a new set of clubs. Drivers vary in the degree or angle of loft, ranging between 9 and 13 degrees. Some clubs are boldly labeled 3½ or 4½. Are there instructions on what to use these clubs for and when? No! Expert advice is required. The golf pro will be helpful, even eager, as he extols the virtues of a particular club. But do not depend on him (or her) alone. Our suggestion is that the Double Bogey Golfer would be wise to consult a physical therapist, a physicist, and a computer specialist for workable advice.

Take the driver. Whatever the manufacturer does to the club, it remains a perilous and wicked club for the Double Bogey Golfer. As mentioned above, no matter the length off the tee he achieves, the ball seldom goes where intended. Few Double Bogey Golfers carry drivers anymore, and if they do, it is mainly for show.

In fact, not only is the above table out of date, it wouldn't apply to the Double Bogey Golfer, inasmuch as no club he carries does what it is supposed to do. For him, the problem of equipment is far greater than for the low-handicap player, who, once he has memorized the table, needs little or no calculating ability. Note how the commentator at a televised golf tournament will instantly detect the club Greg Norman is about to employ.

"A hundred and eighty-two yards to the pin. Six iron, obviously."

"I believe he used a five iron," says the other.

"Probably noticed a bit of wind."

Double Bogey Golfers gnash their teeth at this kind of commentary. Most haven't a club in their bag that would carry a ball that distance. So, in practicality, the Double Bogey Golfer works out his own table of golf club selection. Soon enough he learns to give Goodwill his worthless clubs—usually the driver, then the one and two irons. He is attracted to exotic wedges that are supposed to make the short game a snap. Most now carry six and seven woods with odd-shaped soles that cut grooves in the turf or sweep through rough like a scythe.

Downhill lies are anathema to him, and he'll sometimes blindly select a club, *any* club, for such lies. Some Double Bogey Golfers hit their woods more consistently than their irons and will use a wood for any distance over 53 yards; others find the reverse true —with 300 yards between them and the green, they will select their trusty seven iron, which they have hit fairly well in the past. At least the shot may *look* good, and they can always say afterward that they didn't realize they were hitting into a 30-mile-an-hour wind.

What generally happens, though, is that the Double Bogey Golfer will pursue a process of elimination until he is down to those four or five clubs that work best for him. He may still carry a complete bag, but only because it looks funny to be carrying so few clubs.

By the time he has placed his dependency on those preferred few he will have learned to perform for the benefit of his partners. He'll thoughtfully look over his bag of clubs, run his fingers over several of them, murmur to his partner, "Hmmn, 170 yards I'd say," then choose the club he was going to use in any case, the same club, in fact, that he used for his previous shot.

Not long ago the Golden Means Testing Service queried Double Bogey Golfers on their favorite clubs, with the following results:

CLUB	PERCENTAGE OF USE
7 Wood	22
7 Iron	17
6 Iron	16
6 Wood	14
5 Iron	12
Misc.	19

The vice president of the Golden Means Testing Service, a Double Bogey Golfer himself, played a round using only the above clubs (adding a putter and sand wedge in the place of misc.) and scored a neat 108—three strokes better than his average. He thereupon recommended to manufacturers that they add such a set to their lines, but as yet they have lacked the imagination to do so. One manufacturer did, however, express interest in the club listed as "misc." He wanted to know whether it was a wood or an iron, its loft angle, its shaft length and swing weight, and whether, perchance, it was one of those Carborundrum-shafted and boron-headed clubs the Japanese were making.

From time to time, on a dare or bet, golfers will play an entire course using only one club and a putter. It is a recognized type of play, known as the One Club Event, the rule being that each player must use the same club. But the mystical and visionary Stanley Doyle is the only golfer in the Western Hemisphere who, after three full seasons of experimentation, decided thenceforth to use only one club for regulation play. He rejected all others.

Of all the clubs in his bag (at the outset he was carrying eight

Soon enough he learns to give Goodwill his worthless clubs ...

more than the prescribed 14) he was most consistent with his five iron. On the fairway he generally hit it 135 yards with a nice-looking loft. It struck him that his tee shots with a three wood seldom traveled farther than that—but with the three wood he usually sliced, hooked, or topped the ball. One day, ignoring the hoots and jeers of his playing partners, he took to driving with his five iron. The ball landed three times out of four smack in the middle of the fairway between 130 and 140 yards out.

He did some quick figuring. On a 400-yard par-four hole, three five-iron shots put him either near the green or on it. From there he could hole out in a maximum of three, thus achieving his double bogey, not to mention an occasional bogey. The only birdie of his entire playing career of 11 years came when his third five-iron shot trickled into the hole from 135 yards away—on a 392-yard, par four!

Doyle discovered somthing else. Of all the clubs he tried for pitching and chipping, it was also the five iron that worked best for him. Something about the feel, the shaft length, the loft, gave him a sense of comfort and confidence. So he used the same club for pitches and chips. In common with other golfers of his ilk he had great trouble in bunkers. Why not the five iron? It worked!

Understandably, he wondered if he would have equal success on the putting green with the same club. After a couple of hours of practice he found that he could play a gentle little pitch and run on the green close enough for a tap-in, or close enough for his partners to declare it a gimme.

Something else happened. By employing only the five iron, his handicap tumbled from 35 to, in one season, 29. Soon enough he was playing in the 90s with regularity. He moved right out of the double bogey class into the bogey golfer category. Time, he decided, to reveal himself. He stopped carrying the full bag and marched around the course with his five iron tucked nonchalantly under his arm. The matter came to the attention of the club pro. Doyle's prowess with the five was having its effect on the other double bogey club members and a good many of the lower-handicap members as well. Several with 16 and 15 handicaps challenged Doyle to One Club matches, using *their* favorite clubs. Doyle, a canny fellow, accepted only five-iron matches, and won all with ease. The fever spread. The membership informally voted to include a One Club Event on the tournament schedule, knocking out the mixed foursome event followed by a fashion show, thus angering the wives. The pro was further disturbed when he discovered that sales of clubs and bags at his shop were dropping drastically. The run on five irons failed to make up the losses. Golf cart rentals skidded downward. Teen-agers, used to cadging golf balls lost in rough and water, complained of hard times.

The pro requested a plenary session of the club's board of directors and acquainted that august body with the extent of the damage caused by Doyle's five iron. Doyle's handicap had dropped to 19, and it very much looked as though he would win the Class C championship of the club in a walk.

The rules of the game were consulted and, to the board's consternation, limitations on how *few* clubs a player was allowed to carry were nowhere to be found.

The chairman of the greens committee had been forewarned and had brought along a report, kept secret until he was called upon. His report read:

> On July 17, during twilight hours, the greens keeper examined several of our greens to see if the use of five irons for putting was having adverse effects on the putting surfaces. With the use of plaster casts it was clearly shown that blade marks on the green came from a five iron. Even the number "5" was visible on one of the plaster casts, along with the maker's trademark. It has been ascertained that the five iron used by member Stanley Doyle is responsible for the unusual (though not visible to the naked eye) marks on our greens. It is the opinion of the greens keeper that the minute irregularities caused by Doyle's five iron on putting surfaces is responsible for the rise in handicaps of our three scratch club members. All three have complained of frequent three-putting of late.

The shocked board of directors adopted a resolution to the effect that only recognized and approved putting clubs could henceforth be used on the greens. Also approved by voice vote was an addendum to the club rules on sportsmanlike conduct. "Carrying only one club," the resolution stated, "for an 18 hole round is hereby forbidden, with the exception of a One Club Tournament, to be held only at the discretion of the club president. It is the feeling of the board that a one-club player violates the spirit of the game, as well as its long-standing traditions. Any member breaching this rule will be brought before the membership committee, and, if it is their will . . . "

Doyle bowed before the new rule. He took to carrying a putter along with his five iron. Nevertheless, he was brought before the membership committee in a hearing that lasted three hours before a compromise was reached. Doyle would be allowed the use of his five iron only on fairways and in rough, but never closer than 100 yards from the green. On tees, with the exception of the par threes, he must use woods.

Doyle gave in. He began to use his full set of clubs again, with a resultant rise of his handicap to 32, something a former 19 always finds hard to accept.

Then an inspiration came to him. He located a custom golf club maker, a semirecluse who lived in the woods 15 miles from Walden, Massachusetts. Pledging the club maker to secrecy he ordered a special set of clubs. They were finished in one month's time. The "woods" were actually five irons, the blades cunningly enameled over in a persimmon wood shade. The putter had a standard blade, but the shaft was five-iron length. The irons were investment cast, and the set was stamped "2" through "10." But each and every one was a five iron. The set came in a special bag fitted with a sloping bottom, so that when they jutted out of the bag, the clubs all appeared to be of different lengths.

In almost no time at all, Doyle had driven his handicap down to 21 and all would have been well, except for an unforeseen circumstance. As he played one day with the chairman of the membership committee, that gentleman left his nine iron on the previous green. "Mind if I borrow yours?" he asked Doyle, and before the ashenfaced Doyle could demur, the "9" was taken from the bag and stroked toward the hole, a mere 50 yards away, by the chairman of the membership committee. His shot sailed 70 yards past the green and came to rest under a car in the the garage of a house adjoining the golf course. An unplayable lie.

"That never happened to me before," the suspicious gentleman said, carefully examining Doyle's "nine iron."

Doyle lost his membership.

11 THE PITCHING WEDGE

THE PITCHING WEDGE is regarded with suspicion even by good golfers. Some will do anything to avoid it. They will play a nine iron flat, hoping for the best. They will play a seven-iron pitch-and-run, preferring in effect to kick the ball on the green rather than lift it. Suddenly even these good players are Double Bogey Golfers, sharing the same paralysis when faced with an itsy-bitsy, 30-yard pitch to the green.

Yet the pitching wedge is such an easy club to use.

All that is needed, really, is a left arm with the kind of control that Isaac Stern has in his wrist and fingers, a right with the serve of Ivan Lendl, and the muscular coordination of Joe Montana.

Observe the instrument. It is about the shortest club in the bag. It has a pronounced bend in the blade. One might even consider it wedge-shaped.

There is a reason for that. Mankind, struggling through the millenia, eventually figured out that the greater the angle applied by a striking force to a spherical object, the greater the loft that is achieved. This discovery was a breakthrough as important as the invention of peanut brittle.

Therefore, the pitching wedge has been designed to send a golf ball into or nearly into orbit when struck with appropriate force. Is there anything more thrilling in golf—except, of course, a good drive, or a good fairway wood shot, or a good middle iron, or a successful blast from the bunker—than to hit a high, soaring wedge, watch it float into the stratosphere and flirt with falcons before descending gracefully eight inches from the pin?

In addition, the good players manage to put backspin on the wedge and other iron shots. Forget that. For the Double Bogey Golfer, there is no such thing as backspin.

The trouble is that most golfers want to help natural law. They cannot bring themselves to believe that the angle of intersection equals the angle of loft. They are doubters, skeptics, unbelievers. And so they try to *push* the ball upstairs, or *lift* it upstairs, unwilling to let the laws of nature operate in a normal manner.

The end result is catastrophic.

Watch the Double Bogey Golfer on this 30-yard pitch shot. He grimly advances to the ball, nervous because a good pitch will put him on the green in three, and if he two-putts he will have a splendid bogey instead of his usual two- or three-over.

He stands over his pitch shot. Then he steps away.

"Are we playing winter rules?" he wants to know.

The question is received with the scorn it deserves.

The Double Bogey Golfer sighs and looks at the ball. He looks at the flag. He looks at the ball again and looks at the flag again.

"Goshsake!" somebody says. "There's a foursome behind us."

Finally he lines up, grasping his club in a death vise, the rubber bulging from between his fingers. He brings his wedge back as far as possible and swings down, teeth clenched, elbows flying, muscles bulging. At the very last instant, he comes up on the ball—head up, shoulder up, wrists up. He is trying to *lift* the damn thing.

One of three things invariably happens; the ball shanks far to the right, in darkest rough; it dribbles 10 feet down the fairway; or it is sculled, running like a scared squirrel over the green, coming to rest in a far-side bunker.

The Double Bogey Golfer starts screaming.

"Goodness gracious me!" he yells.

Gone are his visions of the bogey. He will be lucky to hole out in seven.

It is, as the great philosophers have observed, man's lot to make easy things hard. By rights the pitching wedge should be one of the Double Bogey Golfer's most potent weapons. All it needs is the kind of practice that the aforesaid Messrs. Stern, Lendl, and Montana have brought to their performances. The pitching wedge re-

At the very last instant, he comes up on the ball. . . . He is trying to lift the damn thing.

quires no great strength to use. All that is needed is a little finesse, and a little confidence in a basic law of nature (angle = loft). A little practice, no more than four or five hours a day, will then groove a swing that gives nice contact with the ball. The basic thing is to sweep through the ball rather than try to lift it or guide it.

The use of the wedge is contingent upon the fairway lie, as almost anyone can figure out. The Double Bogey Golfer should never use the wedge unless the ball is sitting pretty on grass. If it is in a hole, forget it. Use an eight iron. If the ball is on a bare spot, zing it down its predestined path with a seven iron. Recognize your limitations.

But if conditions are ideal, then grab the pitching wedge. Don't worry about stance, open position, closed position, 60 percent of your weight on the inside of your left foot, and the other arcane things through which the teaching pro drives a Mercedes-Benz and drives the Double Bogey Golfer to near-insanity. There are only three things to remember for the chip shot. Don't bring the club too far back. Sweep through the ball in the direction of the flag (if you take a divot, fine; if you don't take a divot, fine); and follow through.

So now observe the same Double Bogey Golfer on the same kind of 30-yard pitch shot. He has read this chapter. He advances to the ball with infinite cockiness. This time he asks no silly questions about winter rules. He lines up. He brings his club head back, not too far back. He swings down, right elbow nicely tucked in. He follows through. Then he watches a sculled ball run like a scared squirrel over the green, coming to rest in the far-side bunker.

The goddam stupid jerk is *still* trying to lift the ball.

12   THE TEE

~~~~~~

To MOST GOLFERS the tee is a mere sliver of wood or plastic, a humble and purely utilitarian object upon which to place a golf ball preparatory to hitting a drive. That and nothing more. Which shows how little they know.

It so happens that the tee not only has a secret life of its own. Correctly used, the tee can also take strokes off the game. Those who do not realize this are missing one of the more subtle points of golf.

Indeed, the tee is to a golfer as the reed is to virtuosos of the clarinet, the bassoon, and the oboe, not to mention the English horn, the saxophone, and the corno di bassetto.

Reeds are all-important to players of wind instruments. Oboists and bassoonists spend half their lives searching for the perfect reed. They have home workshops where they putter for days on end, cutting and shaping small pieces of bamboo. They·walk through life with bamboo reeds hanging from their mouths like the fangs of the saber-toothed tiger. They are constantly sucking reeds so that the material can achieve proper pliancy and obedience. They are always on the search for new reeds or new types of reed. Among woodwind players there is no other topic of conversation.

The Double Bogey Golfer regards—or should regard—the tee in the same way woodwind players regard their reeds. After all, he needs all the help he can get. The peculiar nature of his swing is such that his drive is thrown off by the least variation or imponderable. He needs plenty of equipment. If the grass around the driving area is high, a short tee will not get the ball into orbit; the golfer will merely be sending a huge clump of grass toward the target, while the ball itself dribbles disconsolately a few feet down the fairway. If the ground around the driving area has no grass at all, a long tee will be responsible for a 75-yard skyscraper.

That common little tee, which so many golfers take for granted, is a very important factor to the success and spiritual well-being of the high handicapper. Wealthy duffers have been known to search the world over for the perfect tee. They have agents in foreign lands everywhere; they will drop everything and fly to Zaire upon receipt of news about a tee of hitherto unknown characteristics. Nobody has as yet encountered the ideal tee, the tee of tees, but the search continues.

Tee manufacturers have not been without imagination in this search. There are wooden tees and plastic tees, in various colors, white and yellow and red predominating. Shapes vary. Some tees look like toothpicks, others, like a Ping-Pong ball cut in half. The variety of tees on the market is indeed bewildering.

What is he to make of all this?

As in any activity of life, there are various schools of thought on the subject. Some Double Bogey Golfers insist on a matched set of bamboo, on the theory that what is good enough for a great oboist is good enough for them. Others disagree. To them, the only viable tee has to be made of the Brazilian pernambuco, the same wood that went into the making of the great Tourte violin bow.

Another school insists that only the rare or precious metals will do. Admittedly, those are expensive. But a tee made from platinum with a head consisting of a scooped-out diamond on which the golf ball can rest is claimed to have the kind of whip that no wooden or plastic tee could begin to duplicate. (Archaeologists recently unearthed a platinum and diamond tee from the tomb of Amenehet III, the great Middle Kingdom ruler. That is one virtue of platinum and diamond: durability. Amenehet's woods and irons, and of course his golf bag, have long since dissolved into rust and dust.)

One limitation of the platinum (or solid gold) tee is that it drives the owner's insurance rates up. There are those who maintain that the obvious advantages of the platinum (or solid gold) tee do not compensate for this limitation. It is a fact that the game can come to a halt while the frantic golfer searches for his $1,250 tee on those occasions he pops it far away. It is suggested that, to speed the game, owners of these tees carry a mine detector.

Some have experimented with a solid diamond tee, but that has proved impracticable. Too brittle. Tees made of solidified sunflower oil, specifically aimed at the Double Bogey Golfer with a high cholesterol count, were found to have a tendency to melt in the sun. Chocolate is a recent development. The golfer can eat these when he gets hungry, though they, too, have a tendency to melt in the sun. Graphite tees are the latest thing, and they have an added advantage in that, if the point is sharp enough, the player can also use them to enter his score.

The tee hunt goes on.

Experimentation has revealed certain facts about the tee in relation to the Double Bogey Golfer. For grass measuring .75 inches high, a tee measuring 2.7843 inches from tip to crown is the ideal. It should be inserted in the earth .944 inches from the tip. For grass 1.24 inches high, the ideal tee is 3.001 inches high. Charts and gauges are available for various grass heights and corresponding tees. The better tees have a Plimsoll line indicating how deep they have to be inserted.

The temperature of the earth has much to do with this matter (this is a *very* recent development, still under study), and it now seems desirable to add a thermometer to your bag to take the temperature of the ground off which you are hitting. It has been found out that cold earth contracts the tee, warm earth expands it. Consequently, certain modifications as to depth of insertion are necessitated. The whip of the tee is also affected by temperature changes. Using a formula obtained from Planck's constant, you can work this out for yourself.

Certain Double Bogey Golfers need a tee that is as much as five or six inches long because of the idiosyncratic nature of their swing. Those tees are not easy to come by, especially in the rarer woods or metals. In this case, it is necessary to make your own, or order them handmade.

The choice of tee material in relation to the Double Bogey Golfer varies from player to player. To each according to his needs. As with clubs, all golfers use those that are (they fondly think) tailored to their specific needs. Some flavor clubs with a great deal of whip. Others are happy only with telephone poles. Some golfers need heavy clubs, others light ones. It therefore stands to reason that the tee should complement the club.

Those with heavy clubs that have little whip need a corresponding tee—one that is heavy and has little whip. Tees made of lead are recommended in this instance.

Whatever the decision about tees, a matched set is needed. These can come in a llama-lined case, complete with ruler and gauges, that can be attached to the belt. If you look silly on your hands and knees, measuring the length of grass and then selecting the appropriate tee, let them laugh. When your score plummets from 118 to as little as 115, the laugh will be on you. A tee is the key.

13   ON PUTTING

~~~~~~

PUTTING IS WHERE you throw away the book. Every authority on golf says that you must find your own solution to the problem of tapping the ball from hither to yon—yon being a hole on the green about four inches in diameter, but perceived from hither as being about one-third inch in diameter.

For the purposes of putting, you can forget about left hand, right hand, flying elbows, and reverse angles or hinges. If you feel comfortable putting while standing twinkletoes with your back to the cup, go to it. Your pro will merely smile his approval. He too has been brainwashed into the belief that anything goes in putting.

This freedom, this all-encompassing permissiveness, leads to some of the most interesting stances ever seen outside the classrooms of the Bolshoi Ballet. It can be argued that Arnold Palmer has done more harm—aesthetically, at any rate—than any golfer in the history of the game. For years the golfing public watched Palmer and his famous stance on television. There he stood, knock-kneed, elbows and forearms horizontal with the plane of the earth, wrists locked into position at an impossible right angle. He looked like the scarecrow in *The Wizard of Oz.* But he was sinking those long putts; no doubt about it. So everybody rushed to imitate him.

Or to go him one better.

The result has been a collection of stances that defy the normal rules of structural anatomy. There are golfers who putt in *demi-plié,* feet in fifth position, arms *en attitude.* There are those who point the left foot in the direction of the hole, place the right foot several yards in the rear, grab the putter well down on the shaft, and move the ball with a masterly stroke of the index finger. The variety is endless; there are crouchers and ramrods, stoopers, inside-out swingers and outside-in swingers, swayers, jabbers, twitchers, measurers, those who try it by science and those wedded to instinct. And they have clubs to match: straight clubs, bent clubs, clubs with offset heads, clubs with heads the size of a matchbox and others with a blade big enough to use as a plough.

But, alas, nothing seems to work very well.

Nothing can diminish a man like putting—the Double Bogey Golfer especially. Suddenly he shrinks when addressing one of those 18-inch testers. He stands there in shock, visibly growing smaller and smaller. Finally he makes a futile, slow-motion push at the ball and it moves exactly eight inches, not quite halfway to the cup.

Many thoughtful observers have noticed a reverse factor. If it is true that the Double Bogey Golfer is always short on his 18-*inch* putts, he is also invariably long on his 18-*foot* putts. He worries and worries over the ball, then gives it a determined shove that would move planets. The ball skitters 12 feet past the hole. This too-little, too-much factor is known as the McHeisenberg effect. McHeisenberg, a former student of Woozler, actually worked out a definitive formula for this phenomenon.

William Shakespeare noticed the McHeisenberg effect as early as 1607. Famous is the remark he made while playing a round with Sir Francis Bacon on his, Will's, home course at Stratford-upon-Avon. Sir Francis, who had one of the keenest minds of all time— and, as is well known, also wrote most if not all of the Shakespeare plays—watched his partner closely. All of Will's short putts were hanging back, and his longer putts overran the cup by 12 feet.

"What unaccustom'd cause propels it thither?" Shakespeare finally asked in sheer desperation.

"I know not," answered Sir Francis, "but 'tis a cause for pity riding the blast like a new-born babe."

Then Shakespeare missed an eight-inch putt and, regrettably, lost his temper.

"Whoreson caterpillar!" he yelled at the ball. "Gor'bellied knave! Fat chuff! Vile-standing tuck!"

Sir Francis was amused.

"Fie, Will," he said. "Angels and ministers of grace defend us! Such language have not I heard to now, betwixt the old moon and the earth. How much art thou shrunk! Thy ignominy sleep with thee in the grave, but," Sir Francis added generously, "not remember'd in thy epitaph."

Naturally great minds have confronted the problem of how the Double Bogey Putter can be helped. "Aye," said MacTeague. "They're naught so wretched as those who fidgin-fain with the cleek over the ball. Oh, would some power give us the gift to strike the ball braw an' true."

Even MacTeague had no ready answers. For a while he recommended a diet of haggis and Scotch whiskey. "Food fills the belly an' keeps us livin'," he advised. He strongly recommended haggis because it lies so heavily on the stomach that it forever stabilizes the golfer's center of gravity. With a midcenter cargo of haggis, and the consequent stability, the golfer would be like those dolls that always return to the same position when pushed.

"Good Scotch drink," MacTeague went on, "heats the veins, fires the blood, and removes the care." It was MacTeague's belief that the whiskey would serve as an anti-inhibitory factor. He claimed that eight four-ounce drams of Scotch, carefully measured, before the morning round would make the Double Bogey Golfer approach his putts with relaxation, merriment, and none of the tension that normally afflicts him when he is on the green.

But, according to contemporary reports, what happened was that the golfers ended up seeing various combinations of balls and holes—never just one each. The result was that they would putt the right ball to the wrong hole, laughing uncontrollably as they did so. There was no doubt that for a while the golfers at Frither Glen were the happiest, most relaxed, least inhibited in all Europe and the American colonies. But there also was no doubt that seven-putt and eight-putt greens were not uncommon.

In more modern times various remedies have been suggested. The golfer is urged to think of putting along an imaginary string, or an alley, or a turnpike. Sounds simple—but not for Double Bogey Golfers, those hitchhikers on the fairways of life. The string twists, the alley turns back on itself, the turnpike leads to nowhere.

One thing seems clear enough, however, and it lies in the nature of the golf ball. Just as the golf ball *wants* to slice, just as it is in the nature of the golf ball to slice, so it does not *want* to drop into the cup. Perhaps this is the result of certain genetic factors in the golf ball, or perhaps it is in its subconscious. Whatever the reason, the golf ball has a horror of the cup on the green. It might be that it thinks it is being sent back to the womb and therefore resists hysterically. Or it may be that golf balls suffer from a mixture of acrophobia, the fear of heights and falling, and cavophobia, the fear of being confined in a small space.

On top of all that, most golfers do not have the psychic authority, the aura of mental determination, to dominate the golf ball. Scratch golfers manage. They *order* the ball into the cup, and their will is stronger than the golf ball's. Thus the ball, however reluctantly, obeys. But just as a wild animal scents fear in some people, and is thereupon aroused to a frenzy of attack, so the golf ball senses when the Double Bogey Golfer is frightened, and immediately takes command.

For the Double Bogey Golfer, then, there is no point in following the basic rules of putting, such as keeping the blade square with the ball in the direction of the cup and firmly striking through. For the golf ball and not the blade of the putter is in command. It will go its own way, well knowing who is the master.

It has been recommended that the double bogeyer bathe himself in expensive colognes and perfumes to disguise this scent of fear. That, however, works only when the ball is exceptionally stupid, and most golf balls are anything but stupid. They know fear when they smell it, and no amount of perfume will hide it. This is because fear is psychic. It goes down very, very deep—infinitely deeper than anything an atomizer can conceal.

There is, fortunately, a way to help the Double Bogey Putter. It takes a little time, but the results are encouraging for those who want to lower their score.

Research has shown that plants respond to loving treatment. There have been monographs and books on the subject. Plants are happier and grow better when the owner speaks to them, sings to them, surrounds them with music, envelops them in an aura of

. . . the golfer and his half-dozen balls should be inseparable.

love. Now, it has been learned, golf balls react exactly the same way. They too respond to loving treatment, to a point where they can overcome their instinctive acro- and cavophobia.

The Double Bogey Putter must select, say, a half-dozen golf balls and reserve them exclusively for putting. *Never, never use them for driving.* One does not smite the object of one's affections. Smack them hard off the tee, and all the good work will be undone. The ball will think it is being punished and, resentful at its treatment, will immediately revert to its natural state.

What the golf ball will not do in fear, it will do for love. Consequently, the golfer and his half-dozen balls should be inseparable. They must always be carried in his pocket and constantly handled and caressed. He must sing them to sleep with a lullaby and wake up several times during the night to make great ado over them. They should be surrounded by music—gentle music of love (the Ignaz Friedman recording of Chopin's E flat Nocturne, Op. 55, No. 2, is especially admired by golf balls).

Think of them as *your* golf balls and they will think of you as *their* golfer. They will then be happy to obey you, eager to seek out the cup from the farthest point on the green.

14 GRACE UNDER PRESSURE

As SOON AS the Double Bogey Golfer picks up a club and takes a practice swing, the mark of Cain is upon him. He knows it and everybody in the vicinity knows it. It will do no good attempting to disguise what nature hath wrought. Bravado, false bonhomie, or nervous laughter only make things worse.

Things are not so bad when you play with others of your kind. But there will come a time when you find yourself part of a foursome of tigers—long-ball hitters, scratch players. Then it will be seen what kind of man you are.

Of course, it is not often that the Double Bogey Golfer finds himself in such august company. But he can walk into a situation where a threesome has to be filled out. There are also certain club tournaments where duffers are coupled to experts, to the misery of both.

Why a 34-handicapper would ever want to play along with par shooters in the first place is a study in masochism that only the

Freudians can figure out. Death wish? Self-hatred? Exhibitionism? Adolescence triumphing over the superego? It is all most peculiar. Yet it is a fact that the Double Bogey Golfer desperately yearns to tag along with the big boys.

Any country club sees the Double Bogey Golfer hovering nervously in the background while foursomes are being filled out. He may be a great tycoon who can buy and sell everybody in the club, and the club itself for that matter. But here he is only a 34-handicap golfer. It is his fate. When he was a kid, he was the last one to be picked for the sandlot game, and he was put in right field, where he would do the least damage. Everybody then knew him for what he was, and times have not changed.

One of the pathetic sights of the universe is to observe him off to the side, gleaming in his new checkered slacks, handsome in a new horizontally striped shirt, cap tilted at a rakish angle over his right eyebrow, new shoes perfectly polished, sweat cloth hanging at the rear of his belt: all dressed up and no place to go. He stands there hoping to be invited into a foursome. Some hopefuls express their desire by becks and nods. Some offer come-hither smiles. Some feign nonchalance. Some have a defiant I-don't-care look. Some are deadpan stoics, hoping against hope. A few carry the battle to the front line. "Anything open, fellows?" Some have actually attempted bribery, though that seldom works.

Usually if he waits long enough, he is chosen. Then what does the Double Bogey Golfer do? Does he volunteer to hit first? Or does he wait until the other three players have hit away?

There is disagreement on the subject. Hieronymus X. Dingle, in his little brochure, *Meisterpsychologischequellenexlikongeschichtenfassungsschwanksammlungpraxishistorie das Golf,* strongly advises the Double Bogey Golfer to hit first. It is his contention that watching three monsters hit 250-plus yards down the middle will provide an inhibitory factor from which he will never recover. In his madness, the Double Bogey Golfer will try to get equivalent distance, ending up you-know-where. Go first, urges the Herr Doktor Professor. Hit your modest hit, smile your modest smile, and make way for your betters.

J. B. Toskiflick disagrees. Toskiflick's view is that the longer the

Double Bogey Golfer puts off the fatal moment, the better. No matter what, he is in a pickle. When he walks to the tee he knows, and everybody knows he knows, and he knows that everybody knows he knows, that he is going to make a bloody fool of himself. So put it off, urges Toskiflick, as long as possible. Try to control the pumping of your heart (yoga exercises are recommended), and breathe deeply. But don't hyperventilate.

There is a big literature on the subject, but no consensus. As often as not, in real life, there is no choice. In almost all cases the unwelcome guest at the feast watches humbly while the gorillas go off, and then makes his own minuscule contribution. Of course, what with a crowd of interested onlookers watching in fascinated horror, the minuscule contribution invariably is a slice out of bounds.

A certain protocol must be observed when playing with experts. It is not that the weak player must continually knuckle his head, and scrape deferentially to his superiors. This, after all, is America, where, according to the Declaration of Independence, all men are created equal. But, Declaration or not, the Double Bogey Golfer simply cannot associate with his companions in this foursome. The disparity in proficiency is too great for him to meet them on equal terms. If there is no aristocracy of birth in the United States, there is, willy-nilly, an aristocracy of talent. All men, in that respect, are not created equal. Not when one player with a driver and a seven iron is on the green in two, while another, on the same hole, with his driver, three wood, five iron, six iron, and pitching wedge is barely there in five.

The other players, on the rare occasions they mess up a shot or miss a 25-foot putt, are entitled to say "Oh, shoot," or something similar. The Double Bogey Golfer, on the other hand, must keep his mouth shut, speak only when spoken to, tend the flag, repair spike and ball marks, applaud good shots. He is there on sufferance. It is only natural that he should offer his three companions cigarettes, tees, ball markers, chocolate bars, chewing gum, a thermos of coffee, perhaps a nip of something stronger on a cold day. They will appreciate it.

If the Double Bogey Golfer is humble in these surroundings, he has much to be humble about. It is a law of nature that he plays at his worst among his betters. His usual 105 ascends into the teens: 115, 118. Or higher. He is always in the rough or in the trap, his patient companions standing by and regarding the entire spectacle in awe.

Nobody except another Double Bogey Golfer could begin to describe the sheer terror that takes possession of him when his game has gone off. The devil is pushing him, guiding his arm and his left side, and he does things he knows are idiotic. He can't keep his head down; every second shot is a shank or a scull; his arms literally tremble as they address the ball. Not one shot works the way he wants. That is sad but true: *not one single shot!*

A madness seizes him . . .

A less determined man would plead sudden illness and walk off, never to return. Not so our hero. A madness seizes him, and in a kind of delirium he staggers through the round, his face fixed in a rictus of dread, the tortures of the damned in his soul. Flopping over the course like a mired mastodon, jabbing at the ball the way Ahab poked his harpoon into Moby Dick, he somehow manages to remain his own man.

If that is not grace under pressure, nothing is.

ETIQUETTE

GOLFING'S CODE OF conduct was once summarized by Mac-Teague. "Ye shall not play," said the sage, "to harry, hamper, or to hurt them as play along with ye, aforeye, or behind." A subsequent injunction of the master's is also considered a reference to the etiquette of the game. "Do ye little harm to the Earth."

The Rules of Golf are quite specific about demeanor. "No one should move, talk, or stand close to the ball or directly behind the ball or the hole when a player is addressing the ball or making a stroke." It is also unwise to interpose yourself between the ball and the hole, for this will place you in harm's way and, in match play, will forfeit the hole should you be struck by an opponent's ball. So ancient is this code that reference to it is made by Chaucer in *The Gowfer's Tale.*

> *A parfait gowfer dresseth neate,*
> *He standeth straight upon both feete,*

And moveth nought, nor twitch, nor flutter,
Speake nought, grunt nought, belch, nor mutter.

While both the U.S. Golf Association and the Saint Andrew's Royal and Ancient Golf Club enjoin players to avoid delay, they also caution against hitting "until the players in front are out of range."

"Out of what range?" asks the novice, who seems determined to dawdle on the tee until the front foursome is out of sight.

"Go ahead," the low handicapper will urge the beginner or high-handicap player, even as those before are clearing the ladies' tee. "You couldn't hit them with a cannon."

This appraisal is not meant to shame or belittle the player so addressed—not always. Yet it can have such an effect, for length of drive is often falsely assumed to indicate virility. To diminish a man's drive is to question his machismo. The player thus goaded then steps to the tee with dual purpose. He wishes to belt the ball a mile. He also wishes not to hit the foursome loitering some 190 to 210 yards up the fairway. Torn by this conflict, he executes a duck hook, a whiff, a bobble, or a low screamer that nearly be-heads an innocent occupant of the practice green.

Because the one consistent quality of the Double Bogey Golfer is unpredictable play, he is sometimes guilty of driving into others, not necessarily on the same hole. If he hasn't pushed a ball more than 150 yards all summer, it is unlikely that he will unleash a 225 yarder just when he risks a shot at an occupied green. Of course, that is precisely the moment it happens. According to a survey conducted for the Association of Neighborhood Negligence Attorneys, the median handicap for all golfers guilty of striking other players with a ball is 32. (Significantly, the median handicap of golfers struck is also 32.)

Low-handicap golfers are also guilty of sending their balls into those ahead, particularly when that foursome is composed of high handicappers. But more expert players lay those intruding drives like warning shots from pirate ships. The ball comes to ground some 10 to 15 yards behind the players, then bounds happily amongst them. Most often, this is a pointed petition to be allowed through, for there is nothing "good" golfers enjoy more than sweeping grandly up the fairway as lesser players line the rough in a properly subservient manner.

The rules are quite specific. A foursome searching for a ball in the rough must always let others pass. On most courses, a match that has allowed more than one hole to open between itself and those in front must let the following match through. Troubles arise when one member of the offending foursome (invariably the slowest player) determines that "They shall not pass," even though his companions are eager to oblige.

There is no satisfactory solution to this dilemma, save for one of the laggard foursome to pick up the obdurate member's ball. The following match can then play through, while the search for the missing ball ("It was right there, in the middle of the fairway") is under way. Once the exchange has been accomplished, the ball should be replaced as near as possible to its original position.

From time to time, a Double Bogey Golfer will himself have occasion to play through a match of female novices (most punctilious as a rule) or small children. It is a costly experience. Two extra strokes is the normal price of playing through under the admiring stares of lesser golfers. Determined to match their faith in your superior prowess, you will burden your fragile swing so that it cannot but collapse. Since the Double Bogey Golfer is incapable of hitting just *one* poor shot, the first disaster is always followed by a second, at which point the ladies or children politely avert their eyes (the better to conceal their giggles).

Golf's code of conduct also encourages such actions as will leave the course unmarked by your passage. This includes smoothing and raking traps, replacing divots, and repairing the small craters your balls inflict upon the greens. As a rule, Double Bogey Golfers are most scrupulous in these matters, and with good reason. Consider their panic when confronted by a poor lie that results from another's negligence. However, there are limits, illustrated by the celebrated case of Casper Cranshaw, late of Cold Charity Country Club.

Casper was thought a bit odd when he let others play through while he searched for a divot. But he next took to carrying squares of virgin turf and halting play in order to cut the right-size patches for the fairway. When he added grass seed and a watering can to his gear and reseeded the 14th tee during the Director's Trophy Tournament, the caddies rebelled, the course superintendent threatened to resign, and the committee had no choice but to suspend Casper for the balance of the season.

If the rules of proper conduct count heavily upon tee and fairway, they weigh mightily upon the green. The novice golfer must learn how to hold the pin (preferably from behind and in a manner that prevents his shadow from crossing either the hole or the putter's line) and mark his ball. Note that the marker is first placed directly behind the ball, and only then is the ball removed. When

But he next took to carrying squares of virgin turf and halting play in order to cut the right-size patches for the fairway.

positioning a marker to the right or left, so as to provide a clear path for the putter, first mark the ball in its original position, then measure a club head's distance parallel to the hole and replace the marker at that point.

Traditionally, one does not cross the line of another's putt because there is danger of cutting the turf with spikes. It is also correct to remove your ball from the cup before the next player putts. Most golfers believe this is to prevent a ball from bouncing out of the hole. It is nothing of the kind. Any reader of de Fleurie knows that it is meant to deny the putter advantage of the sympathetic attraction that exists between golf balls (see next chapter).

16 THE SYMPATHETIC ATTRACTION OF GOLF BALLS

〜〜

"TO UNDERSTAND THE golf ball is to understand golf," wrote l'Abbé Antoine de Fleurie in his seminal work, *A la Recherche des Balles Perdues,* published in 1770.

This simple but canny country priest was not the least concerned with composition, covering, or compression of the crude, feather-filled balls of his day. It was not a mechanistic comprehension that de Fleurie sought. He was the very first golf-ball behaviorist attempting to fathom the mysteries of the ball's flight in a manner appropriate to his clerical concerns.

Watching a golf ball proceed in a direction violently at variance with the player's intent, seeing it alter course in midflight, noting its sudden plummet earthward, observing its leap to trap or green, could not but cause a theologically trained mind of the 18th century to suspect an element of intent, choice, or free will on the part of the ball.

Today, we are immune to such suspicion. Science has triumphed

over faith, mystery, magic, and other glorious concepts by which de Fleurie and his contemporaries explained their universe. We reject the naïve patterns of thought that would let us profit from the findings of de Fleurie or later golfers who noted such vital aspects of ball behavior as:
—the Woozler effect;
—the inclination of golf balls to seek cover;
—the inclination of golf balls to avoid the cup;
—their response to affection, understanding, and warmth.
None of these was known or even suspected when de Fleurie began his research.

It is not even fair to say that this pious Frenchman actually initiated his studies. Indeed, they were thrust upon him, for de Fleurie was no golfer. He was, at best, indifferent to the game. His concern was for the welfare of his parishioners in the tiny village of Sainte Héloïse, whose lord, the Baron Bernard Bouf, was the most renowned golfer in all of 18th-century Picardy. The baron's passion for the game meant tragedy for the village. Acre upon acre of fine farmland was seized by the great lord's stewards so that more holes could be added to what was already the most magnificent golf course of that era.

(It is worth noting that the baronial course had little in common with the rude links of Scotland. It was more like a topflight, private club of today—no mean accomplishment in a period predating the lawnmower. Groundsmen with scissors and clippers tended the fairways, while a crew of barbers daily shaved the greens.)

Poor de Fleurie was allowed to state his case for the dispossessed villagers by accompanying the baron on his morning round, a brisk 11 holes. It was while watching the nobleman's three drives from the fourth tee (an initial shot followed by two precursors of the mulligan) that de Fleurie lost his train of thought. He also lost his audience, for the baron went on to complete his round, while the priest stood rooted to the spot. Indeed, he was still there, pondering the significance of what he had seen when Baron Bouf passed through seven hours later on his evening 11.

What de Fleurie had seen is a common phenomenon that millions of golfers observe with little or no wonder. The baron had followed his first out-of-bounds drive with a second *to the identical spot.* For the month that followed, the churchman haunted the course, counting the number of times the phenomenon recurred. Then he closeted himself in his study. Within three weeks he had produced *A la Recherche* and dedicated the work to Baron Bouf.

Arguing that the number of times a golfer sends two balls in succession to the identical out-of-bounds location defies the law of averages, de Fleurie wrote: "The law of averages is not man's law or church law. It is God's law and unbreakable." Concluding in a brilliant, logical blow, he postulated that sympathetic attraction must exist between golf balls and "where one ball goes, others seek to follow."

The work of de Fleurie was unfortunately lost for almost a century until recovered by Athenagorus Andropolis, the lengendary Greek golfer responsible for the game's brief flowering in Macedonia during the late 1850s. Andropolis added considerable evidence to support de Fleurie's contention. He noted the frequency with which members of the same foursome drive near the same spot on the fairway. But more significantly, he found the de Fleurie phenomenon answered a perennial golfing puzzle—multiple entrapment, or the tendency of balls passing over or near bunkers to arrest their flight or alter their course and join another ball already in the sand. By Andropolis's calculations, a golf ball will safely clear an uninhabited trap in 93 out of every 100 instances. Yet, when the trap is occupied it flies over the sand only 72 times in as many attempts.

Andropolis would have joined de Fleurie in obscurity had it not been for the research of Grendel Gander of Montana Mountain State College. Gander's doctoral dissertation devoted to the de Fleurie phenomenon includes a shrewd series of observations on practice balls. On the practice range, he reports, Double Bogey Golfers can be observed hitting 20 or more perfectly respectable drives in rapid succession. Of course, this success cannot be transported to tee or fairway. As Gander superbly demonstrates, it is achieved by the tremendous pull exerted on practice balls by the mass of balls already well out on the range.

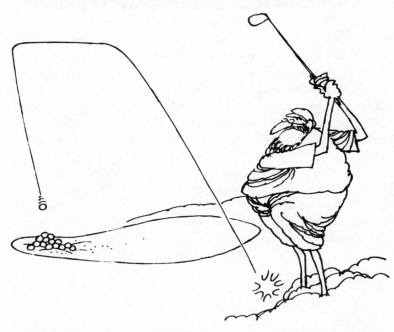

. . . the de Fleurie phenomenon answered a perennial golfing puzzle . . .

While the work of de Fleurie, Andropolis, and Gander illuminates a dark corner of the golfer's world, the average double bogey player is more interested in practical knowledge. He wants to know, "How can the de Fleurie phenomenon help me?"

Believe us, it can.

Indeed it is to prevent an opponent from making use of sympathetic attraction that players remove their balls from the cup and mark and lift them from the far side of the hole. However, unless asked to mark always leave your ball in place when it lies parallel to the putter's line. Thus, it may draw his shot off course.

There are other and more daring applications of the de Fleurie phenomenon. The ultimate "ham-and-eggers," Hec and Hal Stunner, who have rarely been known to lose a wager at Houston's

Purple Sage Country Club, employ the following technique. On a three-par hole, when one brother had made good his honor by being first on the green and close to the pin, the other brother almost invariably will play for the bunker between tee and green. More often than anyone can understand, their opponents' balls join his there. Sometimes, on longer holes that skirt treacherous woods or out-of-bounds areas, a well-placed drive by one Stunner may be followed by a short shot to nearby disaster by the second. Here again, opponents' balls frequently follow the closer and less fortunate drive.

Several long-time victims of Purple Sage's "dynamic duo" have noted that an additional advantage accrues to the Stunners from the de Fleurie phenomenon. Because of wasted drives and penalty strokes, their handicaps remain at a level sufficient to insure victory in 9 matches out of 10.

17　BEARING, DEMEANOR, AND SPEED

BACK IN THE late 19th century when Thorvald MacDougal was eloquently stating the case for Double Bogey Golf, he engaged in a famous debate with C. Barrington Beeches, the great golf critic of the *Aberdeen Examiner*. Beeches maintained that Double Bogey Golfers should be encouraged to take up other amusements. He suggested quoits or kick-the-can. Those who refused to abandon golf, he believed, should be assigned limited playing hours "preferably before seven in the morning or after seven at night."

When MacDougal argued that the Double Bogey Golfer was due the same respect and privileges as the low-handicap player, Beeches responded at length:

> The Double Bogey Golfer is not scorned by other golfers merely for the inadequacy of his play, the damage he does to the course, or the brutal misuse of his equipment. Even the best and most steady of us will, from

time to time, be undone by the course, the gorse, or the weather. No true golfer can withhold sympathy from companion or competitor when he strikes poorly.

The reason we shun the double bogey clan is because we cannot abide their continual distress and preoccupation with their own misfortunes. Those with handicaps exceeding 30 bear themselves without fortitude and languish, through most of the match, between the Slough of Despond and the Firth of Despair. They cannot recall where their balls have lighted, not do they care where others lie. They slight their more able companions in adversity and do not properly regard their feats of competence. They are consumed by envy, self-concern, and self-loathing.

MacDougal struck back, claiming that Double Bogey Golfers held no monopoly on monumental self-concern.

The golfer who plays at or near par is indeed a jovial, albeit condescending fellow when his game holds together and fortune favors his most extravagant efforts. But let him be denied his accustomed length of drive, let his wizardry in sand collapse or his precision on the green falter, and he turns quickly and completely about. Not then does he smile or joke, applaud the shot well made or help to find the hidden ball. He is surly, rude, and an abomination before God. Having fallen from so great a height, the injury to his self-esteem is far more grave and his discontent far more severe than any manifest by the Double Bogey Golfer.

Beeches dismissed MacDougal's sally by saying, "The Double Bogey Golfer never having tasted the joys of adequacy, is permanently soured, turned like week-old cream. He can be said to be even-tempered, and that temper forever foul."

There is, alas, some truth in Beeches's indictment, for Double

Bogey Golfers at war with their natural games are less than happy companions on the course. Theirs is the voice most often heard demanding, "Where's my goddam ball?" They are grudging in admiration, disconsolate in adversity, and most grievously slow in play.

According to Klemriddle's classic study, *Dimensions of Time in Golf,* all playing time can be assigned to one of the seven following functions:

1. Walking
2. Stroking
3. Practice Stroking
4. Selecting Club
5. Studying Lie
6. Addressing Ball
7. Seeking Ball

The average low-handicap golfer (who shoots scratch through 10) spends less than 5 percent of his time in functions 2, 3, 4, 5, and 6, with the following division of each minute so employed:

2. 7 seconds stroking
3. 5 seconds practice stroking
4. 10 seconds selecting club
5. 20 seconds studying lie
6. 18 seconds addressing ball

But the Double Bogey Golfer engages in functions 2, 3, 4, 5, and 6 for twice as much of his time—a full 10 percent. Furthermore, he walks more, tacking like a sloop back and forth across the fairway and from hazard to hazard. He also spends 585 percent more time searching for his ball (and only 27 percent as much time searching for someone else's). But he is at rest far less frequently, only one-third as often as the low handicapper. It is interesting to note how differently he divides each minute devoted to functions 2, 3, 4, 5, and 6.

2. 4 seconds stroking
3. 10 seconds practice stroking
4. 13 seconds selecting club
5. 3 seconds studying lie
6. 30 seconds addressing ball

Plainly, less skilled players spend a disproportionate amount of time addressing their balls, and Klemriddle found a significant correlation between the duration of a Double Bogey Golfer's address and his handicap. In 43 percent of the cases, the number of seconds devoted to pre-stroke meditation and adjustment (out of every minute of stroking, practice stroking, et cetera) was found to equal exactly the subject's handicap. (In 83 percent of the cases, it fell within four strokes.)

Among classic long-lasting addresses is the famous stand of Ginger Noyle, who was clocked at a full 27 minutes in a bunker on the eighth hole at Hoylake in 1874. Penalized for undue delay, Ginger lost the hole. Although it tends to diminish the magnificence of Noyle's achievement, the truth is that his stroke, when finally taken, did not free his ball from the sand.

More recently, a record of sorts was set by Thoreau Nyquist, a guest at Dunlap Downs outside of Akron. According to members of his foursome, who carefully timed the event, Nyquist spent 6 hours and 32 minutes addressing his 112 shots. His round lasted 10 hours and 43 minutes and while statistics are difficult to gather in this sensitive area, we have not seen the equal of Nyquist's staying power.

Lingering over the ball is indeed the hallmark of the Double Bogey Golfer. Yet this lethargy rarely carries over to his swing, for he is among the swiftest in drawing back his club and often premature in lifting his head. Klemriddle contends: "The high handicap golfer has no real conviction that these preliminary shifts, waggles, and thumps will add to his effectiveness. He hovers endlessly above his ball only to delay for as long as possible the dreadful moment when he must strike and, far too frequently, fail."

Lingering over the ball is indeed the hallmark of the Double Bogey Golfer.

18 RULES OF THE GAME

PERHAPS THE MOST common failing of the Double Bogey Golfer is a permissive attitude toward the Rules of Golf. MacDougal railed against it, claiming such laxity demeaned Double Bogey Golfers as a class. Yet, the characteristic persists. It is typified by a plaintive cry on tee and fairway, in rough and hazard: "Must I count that?"

"Only if you're playing golf," the haughty low handicapper invariably replies. And he is right, for what Double Bogey Golfers often play by mutual consent is near-golf, or demi-golf. Such a phenomenon is rare in other sports. Even the sandiest of sandlot baseball games accord each batter only three strikes and no team is allowed any more than three outs an inning. A foul ball does not register as a hit no matter how near the miss.

The game of golf, as it emerged from the mists of history, was designed to pit man and ball against earth and wind. The ball, in its journey from tee to green, was meant to be directed solely by the player's clubs. When MacTeague was once asked if there were not occasions when a ball might be moved in some other manner, he is alleged to have thought for several hours before replying. "There might well be," he allowed, "and there may be times when it would nay be wrong to shear another man's sheep, glean his grain, or make off with his wife. But I dinna ken any, and I dinna chose to." Nevertheless over the years this hard line has been cracked and certain instances of manual intervention are now permitted.

The Rules of Golf (approved by the U.S. Golf Association and the Royal and Ancient Golf Club of Saint Andrews) are available at any pro shop, and it is best for all golfers to know them. Whether they choose to follow them or not is the concern of their peers and their consciences.

There are, sadly, some golfers who will never be cured of the "mulligan." But a second tee shot taken in place of an unfortunate first attempt is nowhere sanctioned.

Other golfers will inevitably bound from the rough bearing their misdirected drives and invoking "unplayable ball" (allowing a player, at the cost of one stroke, to drop his ball within two club lengths of its original lie). But the double bogey rule bender drops, or even *places*, his ball well off the proper line, clear of trouble, with a clean shot for the green, when the distance from his original lie is greater even than several lengths of Paul Bunyan's brassie. If challenged, he invariably snaps, "I took the damn stroke, didn't I."

Clearly, one cannot grow in golf by slighting the rules. Scores and handicaps are meaningless unless a strict standard is followed. What is more, high handicappers sometimes fudge to their own disadvantage. For example, in the confrontation between high- and low-handicap players, it is the high handicapper who most frequently suggests a mulligan on the first tee.

Now, at no other moment in a round of 18 holes is a "good" player more likely to drive into the rough or out of bounds than on the first tee. A half-dozen practice swings are often insufficient preparation; timing may be off and muscles still tight. Normally, the better player is three times as effective off the tee. Only at the

. . . the double bogey rule bender drops, or even places, *his ball well off the proper line . . .*

start of the first hole are the odds narrowed. How ironic that here the Double Bogey Golfer will invariably choose to fudge, nullifying this tiny edge.

At the authors' home course, Double Bogey Golfers have been seen dubbing their first drives, beseeching a mulligan, and faring no better on their second attempt. Then, when their low-handicap opponent drives out of bounds, they cannot deny him the privilege of trying again. Invariably, he will then hit a clean shot far down the fairway. (It should be noted that the first hole adjoins the practice range, the right rough separating the two. With both the Woozler effect and the de Fleurie phenomenon at work, balls fly out of bounds in astounding numbers.)

Mastering the Rules of Golf is more than a means of learning what is permitted and what is not. The rules provide a framework, a discipline, a way to approach golf as a ritual as well as a sport. And it can work to your advantage. While one is not allowed to break the rules in order to win, it is perfectly permissible to use the rules to break one's opponent.

Perhaps the most pernicious perversion of the rule's intent was recorded by P. G. Wodehouse in his tale "The Letter of the Law." The villain of the piece, Hemmingway, is a tricky legalist. His opponent, Poskitt, survives ploy after ploy to reach the 18th green with the match all square. Poskitt is lying three, with his ball just three inches from the cup. Hemmingway, however, is just three feet away in two. When Poskitt's Wagnerian cough (a perfectly justified tit for an earlier Hemmingway tat) causes his opponent to putt wildly across the green and into the far bunker, the match would seem to have been won. Not so. Hemmingway now reveals his true mastery of the rules.

Poskitt is eager to end the contest and return home in time for a luncheon party his wife is having. To miss this event or even to be tardy would cause him considerable domestic distress. But sly Hemmingway announces his intention of waiting the full five minutes he is allowed before taking his fourth stroke. What is more, he informs the impatient Poskitt, "With my next stroke I shall miss the ball. I shall then rest for another five minutes. I shall miss again."

It is clear to Poskitt that Hemmingway can sustain this performance all day. When he stresses his desire to depart, he is told, "Then, what I suggest is that you pick up and concede the match." Since that would make Hemmingway the winner of the club's President's Cup competition (for players with handicaps over 24), Poskitt sends word to his wife that he will be detained. The word he gets in return is far from encouraging.

The dilemma is resolved and the day saved by a young suitor of Poskitt's daughter. He sends a ball from the practice tee straight into Hemmingway's left leg, just as the latter is addressing his ball. The stricken Hemmingway thereupon drops his club in the bunker, forfeiting hole, match, and the President's Cup.

Rarely is a links lawyer like Wodehouse's Hemmingway an asset to a foursome. However, he can prove of great value when the foursome includes a member whose moral fiber is frayed.

In golf, one assumes the other fellow is not cheating. Often, this assumption is unwarranted. People do cheat (see next chapter) and there are more ways to cheat than there are means to discourage it. Some of the nicest people (in most other ways) are ethically skewed when it comes to golf. As Fetlock and Sherman revealed in their epic study, *Morality on the Links,* men and women who ranked "very honest" or "most honest" or even "saintly" by such tests as "The Dropped Wallet" or "Undercharged at the Supermarket" can earn a rating of "scurrilous" when subjected to "Ball out of Bounds and Player out of Sight."

But the hawk-eyed links lawyer can be counted upon to set things right just when his shifty opponent believes he has stolen an edge. Let the tricky one free his ball from encumbrances in the rough and send the subsequent shot squarely to the green. "Sorry, old man," the legalist calls from across the fairway. "I'm afraid you played out of turn [there may be all of four inches difference in their lies]. You'll have to wait and play another ball. Rule 20-2, you know."

At Blasted Heath, Marvin "Gung-ho" Gillespie was long suspected of snagging his ball out of bunkers, but he avoided his comeuppance until matched against Clarence Judicator in the 1964 Class A championship semifinals. Four times, Judicator saw his opponent's ball heading for sand. But when he reached the scene, there was Gillespie grinning over a ball a full three feet back from the bunker.

On the 14th hole, with the match even, Gillespie's shot to the green fell short, obviously in the bunker. Judicator dashed to the spot. Before Gillespie could arrive, he dropped a dollar bill onto the sand beside the ball. Gillespie, with no alternative save playing the shot from where his ball lay, took sparkling sand wedge in hand and marched onto the hazard. "What's this?" he called, spying the currency. "It's a dollar," he answered himself, and, as Judicator had anticipated, snatched up the bill.

"Ah ha," boomed Judicator. "You lose the hole."

"What?" Gillespie sputtered.

"Before making a stroke," quoted Judicator, filled with proper awe for the law, "the player shall not—" and he rattled through the rule, concluding, "or touch or move a loose impediment lying in or touching the hazard." He paused. "The penalty is loss of the hole."

Such is the use of the law and the value of the legalist.

19   CHEATING

THE DOUBLE BOGEY Golfer is an upright and honest gentleman who never bends the rules, much less cheats. He may be a duffer, but he has integrity. It is a regrettable fact, however, that other golfers have, every once in a great while, been known to cheat. MacTeague, with his dour Scot's pessimism, well knew this, and he sorrowed. "Och," he said, "mankind is unco weak and little to be trusted."

Cheating infuriates the Double Bogey Golfer. And it is especially unfair to him, of all people. If a better player stoops to unethical means, it not only erases the minimal advantage of the Double Bogey Golfer's handicap, it can also cost him a pile of money. For, humble though he may be, the Double Bogey Golfer has been known to get into a nassau where, as the game goes along, there is a press, a double press, a double-double press, and a few side bets here and there. All this can add up. Therefore, he must be constantly on the alert.

Like all golfers, the high handicapper has been exposed to the common or garden variety of cheating. Most common is the character who picks up a ball from the rough, examines it, says "Yeah, that's mine," and replaces it. No golfer in the long history of the game has been known to replace his ball on a worse lie. It sometimes even happens that the ball is replaced on a better lie. Such is the perfidy of man.

Or there is the guy there on the side, in the rough, whistling and looking at the sky while the tip of his toe, or the toe of his three iron, is nudging the ball from behind a clump of garbage onto a nice, raised surface.

The garden variety of cheats can be dealt with easily. A stern look, a shake of the finger—naughty! naughty!—is usually enough to do the trick. There is no call to take out a .38 and shoot the culprit dead. While any jury in the United States would find for the defendant, such action is simply bad form.

But some cheaters are ingenious, and the Double Bogey Golfer must train himself to move suspiciously through a venal world.

To give but one example, it is wise to examine the shoes of everybody in your foursome. You ask why. Did you not see that old James Bond movie where Lotte Lenya extended a poisoned prong from the tip of her shoe and kicked out at the hero? From which resulted the case of Fergus McGonigle.

McGonigle, inspired by the film, hired a master shoemaker to create a right shoe in which a forklike apparatus, operated by the big toe, would sneak forth, gently lift the ball and deposit it where it would do the most good. The apparatus would then retract. McGonigle could perform this act while standing motionless, arms akimbo. Nobody could possibly detect the chicanery. It is true that after a while everybody wondered why McGonigle never had a bad lie in the rough.

Cheating is not necessarily involved with mechanical gimmicks. It can be consummated by the subtlest of means. As Shakespeare says, a man can smile and smile and be a villain. Anything one player deliberately does to throw off another is cheating, and it can be accomplished without violating a single rule, as in the famous

McGonigle . . . hired a master shoemaker to create a right shoe in which a forklike apparatus, operated by the big toe, would sneak forth, gently lift the ball and deposit it where it would do the most good.

game between Johannes Brahms and Franz Liszt at the Wartburg in the Thuringian Valley.

It so happened that Brahms and Liszt had, between them, four of the most phenomenally accurate ears of any musicians in history. What has that got to do with golf? Well, at the 14th hole Liszt found himself two down. Brahms strode to the tee. As he started his downswing, Liszt began to whistle, very softly, the *Ride of the Valkyries*. Brahms topped his ball.

"You know how I *hate* that piece," he snarled.

Liszt looked contrite and apologized. But he won the hole. Brahms simmered. On the next tee, as Liszt was bringing down his driver, Brahms started to whistle, very softly, Liszt's own *Liebe-straum*. And, terrible to relate, he deliberately whistled it half a tone up—in A major. Liszt turned green.

Brahms well knew what he was doing. He and Liszt had absolute pitch, and when a musician with absolute pitch hears a piece of music in the wrong key it is a total shock to his nervous system. Physically, he hears what is impinging on his eardrums—A major, in this case. Mentally, he is hearing the music in its original key, A flat major. Thus, his ears encapsulate a bitonal clash, the effects of which are more devastating than a dentist's drill. Liszt not only missed his ball completely, he was so upset that he could not continue and had to forfeit the match.

"Scheissmeister!" he roared at Brahms.

"Kopfsalatkopf!" Brahms roared back.

"Stümper!"

"Schwindelein!"

"Krummstab!"

"You started it," said Brahms.

They never spoke to each other again.

The things some players stoop to! Golf balls, for example, should be scrutinized with special attention. The Double Bogey Golfer should regard with infinite suspicion any member of a foursome who consistently hits over 550 yards off the tee. It is just possible that a doctored ball is in use. And beware of irons with very thick shafts. Possibly they are Crumm's searching iron.

Whittaker Crumm, who played at Mediocre Meadows, was never known to lose a ball in play. He would grab his thick searching iron, depart into the rough, or even into the deepest forest, and presently would come the yell: "Here it is!" Small minds and mean spirits might question Crumm's unerring eye, but the fact remains that he never lost a ball. It was also noted that he never used his searching iron on the fairway. So what? Linus has his blanket. Crumm had his searching iron.

One day Crumm was having a bad time on the fairways. One of his foursome came up just after Crumm had shanked a ball. "You're not staying down on the shot," he said. "Here, let me show you." Reaching into the bag, he removed the searching iron.

Crumm's face went ashen. His friend tried to get his hand around the two-inch grip. There was absolute silence. The skies darkened. A putt was heard to drop on the distant 18th. All stared at the figure hunched over the searching iron. Suddenly the fingers touched a bump in the leather. Plop, plop, plop. The club head swung open and 18 brand-new Royals fell out of the shaft. Crumm was undone.

Because of microminiaturization, certain types of cheating are getting harder and harder to detect. Keep an eye peeled for Merton's Magic Marker. It looks like the ordinary marker one inserts into the putting green. But a fluoroscopic examination might reveal it to be packed full of transistors, printed circuits, and other electronic goodies, all working together to throw an immense magnetic field over the entire area. Muggeridge Merton invented it, and he used it sparingly. But when the chips were down, as in the Class EE championship at Upsand Downs, he would use his marker. His opponents just could not understand why their three-foot putts consistently missed by a hair. What was happening was that Merton's Magic Marker was exerting such magnetic force that the metal heads of the putters were thrown a shade off line. Then Merton would place his ball down, remove his marker, give it a tiny twist to cut out its magnetic field, put it in his pocket, and address his own putt.

It was Merton's misfortune that a delegation of Russian scientists visited Upsand Downs, and one of them became part of Merton's foursome. Russians, as often as not, have steel caps on their teeth, and the mouth of Vassily Pietrovich Pazzazzky resembled a wrought-iron fence. When Merton activated his Magic Marker, it pulled every tooth out of Pazzazzky's head. There was an anguished scream and an immediate investigation. The keen scientific brains of the Russian delegation soon came up with the answer. At a club meeting it was decided that Merton's punishment, in addition to expulsion, was to be locked up in a room with Pazzazzky for two hours. Pazzazzky was to be supplied with a pair of pliers.

It goes without saying that the higher the nassau and the more the side bets, the greater should the Double Bogey Golfer be on his guard. Never play with a certified public accountant. At the end of the match something like this is going to come out of his mouth: "Let's see," the CPA says, his trained eye scanning the scorecard, "we won the first 9 and you won the back 9, but we took the 18 and you had 2 greenies but we had a greenie and 2 birdies and also 4 skins and you took the first press, but we were two up on the double press and you owe $3 on the side bet on the 14th and then there was the double on the 18th, and let's see you owe us $36." And who is going to argue with a certified public accountant, even though you, with a forced smile, dig in and pay out knowing all the while that you are being taken for a double-entry ride?

No, definitely never play with a CPA.

As a matter of fact, the Double Bogey Golfer should never play with anybody except Double Bogey Golfers.

20 HANDICAPS AND WAGERS

GOLF IS DIFFERENT from other games.

Consider, for example, the ratio between playing area and size of goal. Were that same relationship to exist in basketball (forgetting soccer, hockey, or football) the basket would shrink to the size of a thimble.

Then, there is the handicap system that permits players of varying ability to compete against each other. The true nature of the handicap cannot be comprehended from the narrowly mechanistic means by which it is assigned (averaging the best 10 of a player's last 20 scores and awarding him 85 percent of the difference between that figure and par). The handicap represents something far more profound. Not only is it the game's great equalizer, it is also the basis of one's golfing identity.

Unhappily, there are those who see this only in terms of status. Such a perception can cause a never-ending battle between pride and pocket to rage within the breast of the minimally skilled player.

There are those who will withhold their highest scores to artificially lower their handicaps, surrendering for ego's sake just about any chance of winning a match or collecting a wager.

Indeed, they sacrifice more than that.

A handicap specifies a golfer's natural role and divinely assigned position in the cosmology of the sport. "Ye must play yer own game," MacTeague declared. "The Almighty sets men's limits." The legendary Scot demanded of his disciples (in addition to six feathered balls, a salmon of not less than seven pounds, and 10 shillings a year) that they obey the injunction, "Do not exceed thyself."

It is hardly surprising that Calvinism took root so readily in Scotland, and there are many who contend John Knox would never have won converts to so stern a creed were it not for golf. The Scots understood at once what predestination was all about. The doctrine needed little exposition in church, for it was amply demonstrated on the links.

One must play to the handicap God sets. There is no other way to grow and find understanding in golf. Follow the rules, count all strokes, and post all scores. That is the good and godly way; but it is no path to riches. Even with an honest handicap, a poorer player is unlikely to take a match from a better player and, in the long run, he must lose more wagers than he wins.

Golf is filled with competitive possibilities and various ways of betting on them. But the nassau is perhaps the most common. Let us assume the nassau is being played for one dollar. That means that there are actually three bets involved—one dollar on the first nine, one on the second, and one on the entire round. Nassaus are played by individuals and by teams, at one point a hole (for low ball) or two (plus for low ball, minus for high ball).

But the most insidious aspect of the nassau is the "press." This gives a team that has fallen behind the right to initiate a new bet for the remainder of the nine or 18. The press is automatic in some clubs, when one side is down two or more holes after the first nine (and the automatic press sometimes involves extra handicap strokes for the losing side). There is also the possibility that the team that won the first nine will start out poorly on the back and

One must play to the handicap God sets.

be able to launch a press of its own. And so it goes, making even the "dollar" nassau the potential vehicle for a considerable number of dollars.

For the Double Bogey Golfer, betting is a sure route to poverty. He cannot expect to win money from better players over a prolonged period of time unless he falsely inflates his handicap by failing to post his lowest scores (an act so offensive we dare not comment upon it).

The reason the Double Bogey Golfer cannot win as often as he loses is simply the difference between the way that handicap strokes are given and the way most Double Bogey Golfers play. When a 30-handicapper plays an 18-handicapper, the former gets 12 strokes. In match play, these strokes are given on the 12 most difficult holes (as indicated on the scorecard). But the Double Bogey Golfer rarely loses the most difficult holes by a mere stroke. He loses by two or even three. It is on the *less* difficult holes that handicap strokes would be most useful, but that is where the low handicappers of this world are most unwilling to surrender them.

In June of 1973, the Triennial Congress of Double Bogey Golfers proposed that the present handicap system be replaced. Among the most popular suggested alternatives were systems that granted strokes on the basis of "bottom holes" or "one through" or "player option." The bottom-hole method would award strokes on the least difficult holes. On a first-through basis, they would simply be given on each hole in turn, starting with the first, so that a player receiving seven strokes would get them on holes one through seven. But the congress's real favorite was the player-option suggestion that high handicappers be allowed to decide after a hole has been played whether or not to use one of their handicap strokes.

As a test of the different systems, an average scorecard was selected from among the matches played between Double Bogey Golfers and straight bogey golfers during the four days the congress was in session at the Rushes Ho Hotel outside of Wheeling, West Virginia. The results are shown in Table 1 on page 132.

The great virtue of the player-option method is immediately apparent. However, all three proposed changes would leave the Double Bogey Golfer better off than he is under the present system. If a dollar nassau (excluding presses) had been played by this twosome, Player B would have lost three dollars with the present method of giving handicap strokes. He would have won one dollar if the first-through system were adopted or two dollars if bottom hole was played. Under player option the Double Bogey Golfer would have collected all three dollars. Obviously, player option is the best system.

However, the U.S. Golf Association would not consider the petition of the Double Bogey Golfers Congress, refusing even to discuss changes. Representatives who returned from the congress fared no better at their home clubs. They were laughed out of golf committee meetings by the low-handicap golfers who dominate such bodies and are motivated by narrow self-interest. In golf as in life, the system seems stacked to let the rich get richer while the poor get poorer.

Hole	Par	H'cap	Player A (18)	Player B (30)	Present System	"Bottom Hole"	"First Thru"	"Player Option"
				TABLE 1	FOUR HANDICAP SYSTEMS			
1.	4	9	5	5	+1*	+1*	+1*	+1*
2.	5	5	6	8	−*	−	−*	−
3.	4	11	5	6	−*	−*	−*	−*
4.	3	15	4	4	−	+1*	+1*	+1*
5.	4	1	6	8	−1*	−	−*	−
6.	5	3	7	7	−*	−	+1*	+1*
7.	3	17	4	4	−	+1*	+2*	+2*
8.	4	7	5	6	−*	+1*	+2*	+2*
9.	3	13	3	4	−1	+1*	+2*	+2*
			(45)	(52)				
10.	4	6	5	6	−1*	−	+2*	+2*
11.	3	18	4	4	−1	+1*	+3*	+3*
12.	4	10	5	5	−*	+2*	+4*	+4*
13.	4	14	8	6	+1	+3*	+5	+5
14.	4	2	5	7	−*	+2	+4	+4
15.	5	12	6	9	−1*	+1*	+3	+3
16.	4	4	5	7	−2*	−	+2	+2
17.	3	16	3	4	−3	−*	+1	+2*
18.	4	8	5	5	−2*	+1*	−	+3*
			91	105				

* Indicates holes on which handicap strokes are given.

SOURCE: *Proceedings of Triennial Congress of Double Bogey Golfers*, June 1973 (mimeographed), p. 749.

21   "HOW I PLAY DOUBLE BOGEY GOLF"

* EDITOR'S NOTE: Jack Burkmiller, a long-time member of Goose Downs Country Club of Herkimer, New York, was selected by the writers as a model exponent of Double Bogey Golf. Playing to a 33 handicap, his methods would seem applicable to the class in general, and would repay study. Burkmiller, an insurance broker, also writes a column "Herkimer in History," for *The Mohawk Valley Sentinel,* a weekly paper distributed free in Herkimer, Mohawk, Ilion, Frankfort, and Golgeville. We have taken the liberty of truncating his remarks when they stray from golf to regional matters.

"FOR MANY YEARS, like most high handicap golfers, I regarded myself as a failure because I could not break into the 90s, much less the 80s and 70s. The day of insight came when I realized that par was forever beyond my reach, and that I must therefore adjust my swing and psychology to the type of game for which I was best fitted. I was midway through a series of 100 lessons with Ed Seeley, the Goose Downs pro, and we worked out a rebate on his insurance in return for canceling the remainder of the lessons. 'Your swing works very well for you,' I told him, 'but only makes my game worse.'

"I determined to evolve my own technique, along with a strategy for playing the par-71, 6320-yard course on which, from the 11th tee, one can see the Mohawk River winding its way through apple orchards and cornfields. Indians once pitched their tepees along these same banks, then lined with birch trees from which they peeled the bark and fashioned their canoes before paddling downstream in stealthy attacks on General Herkimer's fort. . . .

"Contrary to Seeley's advice, I changed my grip from overlapping to interlocking. I carried the backswing approximately three-fifths of the way, upon which I shifted my weight to the big toe of the left foot, digging it firmly into the ground as I came through on a choppy downswing. This is my own swing; I daresay it will not benefit all Double Bogey Golfers. Nor is it a picture-book swing. But, for me, it gets results: a fairly straight 150 yards off the tee with a four wood, 120 yards with long irons, and as much as 80 with short irons. A bit of advice: Getting off the tee is less difficult if not thought of as a drive. Just take the four wood and go for an easy 150 yards. Because of my talent for taking it slow, steady, and easy, I am affectionately known by Goose Downs members as The Turtle. Oddly enough, the name has helped my game rather than the reverse.

"The Goose Downs sixth hole is a 360-yard par four, and obviously impossible for me to reach in two strokes. I therefore separated the hole into zones. (I did this mentally, of course; one doesn't give away one's methods to opponents.) From the tee to 150 yards out was Zone 1; Zone 2 was the next 100 yards, safely past two fairway traps; Zone 3 extended to a hillock (indubitably an Indian burial ground, for our grounds keeper swears he once dug up three skulls while reseeding) overlooking the green, a pleasant little chip shot. There are times when I am tempted to try hitting from Zone 1 to Zone 3, but experience is a wise teacher. Those who will not learn from history are condemned to repeat it, as uh, uh . . . who said that, anyway? In any case, it is my aim to place my shots as closely as possible within the limits of those sectors. If all goes well, I hole out in six, and, with a lucky putt, will sometimes achieve a five.

"I *never*—repeat, *never*—attempt to exceed 150 yards with my tee shot, with one exception, which I'll mention later. Any excess effort, or overstriving, lands me in trouble, as it often does for one of my opponents, Sam Beckwick, whose handicap is 20 and whose scores vary between 92 and 110. Sam won't like my saying this, but unlike him I always turn in my scores. Sam's ego is such that he cannot face having a higher handicap than 20; thus he won't turn in any score higher than 95.

"At nassau, Sam is a patsy for me. Playing the above-mentioned sixth hole, Sam's drive, a boomer of as much as 240 yards, will either land in one of the fairway bunkers, skip into heavy rough, or hit one of the spreading horse chestnut trees on the left edge of the fairway. He'll be lucky to hole out with a six, which means that my own six wins, since on that hole I get a stroke from him.

"Because of my high handicap, and my unusual steadiness, I am much in demand as a partner for nassau foursomes. Club members toss coins to get The Turtle (as they affectionately call me) for their partner. I hope never to go below my 33 handicap. By consistently winning a few dollars per round, I earn back a nice slice of my membership dues.

"I am not immune to trouble, however. No one is. A shanked iron will find the rough, imperiling my double bogey. From the same spot, Sam Beckwick will use his four or five wood, and go for the green. Instead his shot travels farther into the rough, or scars one of the spreading horse chestnut trees. I *never* use a wood from the rough, and seldom from the fairway. My strict rule: When in the rough use a wedge, even when the ball sits up nicely. Should a tree be anywhere close to the line of flight, I aim at least 90 degrees away from it, even if this takes me back toward the tee.

"*The fairway is the place to be.* If off the fairway, *get back.* Never try to hit *over* obstacles. Go *around* them. Remember that on par fours your low-handicap opponent is trying to reach the green in two. You have *four* strokes. If, by chance, you bogey instead of double bogey, regard these as a counterbalance to your occasional sevens. Even the most canny Double Bogey Golfer will land in a bunker now and then.

"Ed Seeley used to give me lessons on exploding from sand. 'It's *easy*,' he'd yell at me in exasperation. 'Why can't *you* do it?' Well, I can't. Either I hit nothing but sand, or explode the ball over the green into the trap on the other side. Before I evolved my double bogey strategy I averaged four strokes per bunker.

" 'Let's be sensible,' I told myself. 'Think through this problem. I am wasting strokes by trying to extricate myself from sand in the standard and approved manner. Let's have some original thinking.'

"I examined all 47 bunkers guarding the 18 greens of the Goose Downs course. The first thing I noticed was that they were designed to be easy to get into and difficult to get out of it. Why was this so? Because from the fairway side they were shallow, and steep facing the green. The answer came in a blinding flash: Instead of aiming the shot for the pin, hit back to the fairway! And, taking two strokes because of landing in sand is much more sensible than taking four.

"Thus, when trapped I now turn my back to the pin and green and, with a seven iron, chip back to the fairway, and thence to the green. Around the club they dub it 'The Turtle Trap Technique.' Nevertheless, I often have the last laugh.

"Sam Beckwick hooted in derision the first time I tried the method. But, as we marched onward hole after hole, The Turtle Trap Technique took its toll on him. On the 14th, he took five shots attempting to explode out of sand four feet below Mohawk River level. When at last, red-faced, his ball was on the green, I merely remarked: 'It's a wise owl who knows when not to hoot.' The saying was not original. Chief Thomas Hawk, a Mohawk who roamed our valley in the early 1700s said it first. The date, I believe, was 1731. Curiously, Chief Hawk. . . .

"Why, I have been asked, do I never, or almost never, use my woods on fairways? Plainly speaking, I regard fairway woods as treacherous. Something about their construction induces anxiety and causes one to look up. Irons get you closer to the ball. When well lofted, they remind me of small shovels. 'Just shovel that ball,' I tell myself. But a wood is not built like a shovel; you simply can't shovel with it. However paradoxical it may seem, I do on occasion hit a fairway wood, but only when I am playing with such precision that it looks as though I'll easily break a hundred. Obviously, that would endanger my 33 handicap.

"It's then I'll hit away recklessly with a three wood, hardly ever failing to top the ball, and getting a roll of no more than 40 yards. Under similar circumstances, I will use my driver at the tee. 'Let's go for 200 yards,' I'll tell myself. I take a full backswing and a lovely follow-through. This causes a muffed drive. But I do this only when I require a triple bogey rather than a double.

"Our worst water hole at Goose Downs is the 15th, a 140-yard par three. The hole looks as follows:

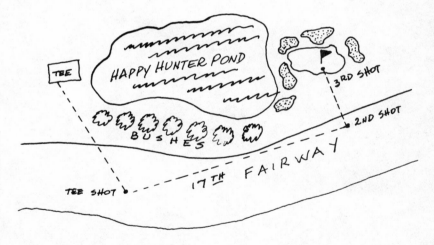

"By referring to the above diagram, it can be seen that my tee shot is played with a six iron to the adjoining fairway (the 17th), that my second shot continues along the fairway of the 17th to a point parallel to the pin of the 15th, and that my third is a simple 30-yard pitch to the green. I normally get down in five on the 15th. Beckwith's tee shot (also a six iron) lands in Happy Hunter Pond four times out of five; not only does this cost him the hole, but loses him hundreds of balls during the year. The rule at the 15th, you see, is that once having hit into the pond, the next shot must again be hit from the tee, with penalty of stroke and distance. Sam's record for the hole is seven lost balls and a score of 26.

"I have found that my method of play makes for an easy, enjoyable round, and while I have the club's highest handicap, I would never trade it for a lower handicap and the unhappiness that goes along with it. I stride along, enjoying the unpolluted air, the views of hill and valley, of maple trees and aged oaks, where once the Mohawks roamed, where once their tepees stood, thin plumes of smoke rising from pinewood fires, while braves worked on their birchbarks, and the squaws. . . . "

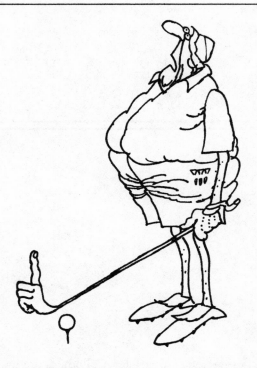

"Plainly speaking, I regard fairway woods as treacherous. Something about their construction induces anxiety and causes one to look up."

22

THE WAY OF
MacTEAGUE

~~~~~~

THESE PORTIONS OF the Frither Glen Colloquies are taken from
the collection presented by the glen's 15th master to King Edward
VII (who, as Prince of Wales, was elected captain of the Royal and
Ancient Golf Club of Saint Andrews) on the occasion of his maj-
esty's coronation in 1901.

▪ ON WOODS AND IRONS ▪

"Earth and wood have a bond beyond man's making," MacTeague
once said, "for the touch of wood to turf is in harmony with
nature's design. But iron," he warned, "comes as an intruder to be
resisted and repelled. The golfing iron, no less than plow and pick,
spade and scythe, means to impose man's will upon reluctant earth.
So I say, it must be gently wielded, with compassion and understanding."

▪ RUB OF THE GREEN ▪

The first master of Frither Glen did not hold with elaborate greens-keeping. In fact, he spoke strongly against it, saying: "I do not fancy trimming and clipping about the hole to smooth away the risk from putting. 'Tis not golf. Talent and skill can carry ye to the green, but once there they count little. Chance rules. And the bump or clump that sends a ball awry tests more than eye or arms. Do not defy the rub of the green; accept it. The drive is driven with strength and cunning, but the putt is sunk by grace."

▪ ON SWINGING THROUGH ▪

"The swing," said MacTeague to his disciples, "never ends."

Just what the master meant by this was not clear. The young men pondered it in their various ways.

"Obviously," declared Derek the Red, a large lump of a lad from Kilmarnock, "he means the swing makes a circle. Ye follow through and around until the club head is back where it began."

"Nonsense," argued Peter Shortputt, an angular and argumentative youth of Glasgow. "He means ye cannot think on one swing alone, but on the total of all the swings ye take."

Merton the Quiet stood mute. He would not side with Derek nor agree with Peter. Finally, he asked, "Could not he mean that the swing must go farther than the arms can reach? It must take the ball at rest and put it to flight, carry it high, keep it straight, bring it to ground, and set it at rest again. And no single swing can be ended until the next begins."

The three brought their dispute to MacTeague the next day and bid him settle it. Each offered his interpretation, Derek proudly, Peter loudly, and Merton hardly at all.

"Ye are none of ye wrong," the sage replied, "Merton least of all. But do I not speak plain?"

They nodded.

"Then why make difficult what is simple? The swing never ends because the swing is in the head and not in the arms."

■ ON SHANKING ■

(NOTE: The true nature of the shank was unknown until recent discoveries by Grendel Gander revealed it to be an acute manifestation of the Woozler effect. The cause is most likely some physical imbalance in the player. Gander has suggested it may be triggered by one's iron level or potassium intake.)

At Frither Glen, the shank was never called by name, but known instead as "that terrible thing." It was considered the final and finest test of golf, for it struck indiscriminately at novice and master alike. From all across Scotland, men brought their shanks to the glen, which enraged MacTeague. "We've no pesthouse here," he railed. "Get ye gone, and take the plague with ye."

But the master could not turn away Brian Longirons Morrison, for the pride of Aberdeen had served and studied at the glen. MacTeague valued the man.

"Can ye rid me of my shank?" pleaded Brian.

"Nay."

"And why not," pressed the shaken golfer, whose hard-driving irons were the delight of his club.

" 'Cause I did not give it to ye."

Brian stared blankly at his teacher.

"Ask me to rid ye of that great, screaming drive or those long irons that please ye so. Those I gave, and those I can take away. But I did not give ye that terrible thing. A more powerful One than I did that." And, without waiting for Morrison's next words, MacTeague strode off.

The next morning, Brian was practicing in the glen a full hour before breakfast porridge. Shot after shot flew true. But then, first one and next another arched off sharply to the right. The man from Aberdeen persisted, and was still at it when MacTeague came by.

Settling himself upon an oak stump, the master watched Morrison work. By noon, the golfer's arms were weary. Came late afternoon, and every stroke was anguish. Yet, Brian swung on. The shank, however, was as stubborn as he.

All the while, MacTeague waited. Evening came, and he rose. "What have ye learned, lad?" he demanded.

Brian shrugged.

"Will ye be back tomorrow?"

Brian nodded.

Now, it was MacTeague's turn to shrug. He did and walked away.

The following morning, young Morrison was again in the glen. He stayed until dusk. As the sun dropped from sight, MacTeague came down to join him. "Now," he asked, "is that terrible thing still with ye?"

"Aye," Brian admitted.

"And what have ye learned?"

Brian had an answer now. "That it will not go away."

"Just so," agreed MacTeague. "Not till it's ready. Ye cannot force it. Ye cannot fight it."

"But why—" Brian began.

"To make the game complete," the old teacher told him. "It would not do for the testing to end just when one's most worthy. That terrible thing is sent to check man's pride, so he can never hold himself to be master of golf."

"But you—" Brian started again.

"Aye, even I," confessed MacTeague, "even I."

"And what do ye do?"

"One does," said the founder of Frither Glen, "that which must be done. 'Tis the first rule of golf. What cannot be overcome must be played out."

▪ ON TEACHING ▪

Many came to Frither Glen to study with MacTeague. Few were allowed to stay. The master chose his students. They did not choose him. And no one offered the chance ever spurned it. But there was, in Dundee, a certain rich man named Beadle, who was determined to learn the game from the sage himself.

Beadle came north. Three coaches carried his trunks and provisions, servants, and female relations. His retinue crowded the nearest inn. The morning after they arrived, Beadle called upon MacTeague. When the master's door remained closed, the wool merchant returned to the inn to sulk. The next morning, he went again. This time, he brought a servant whom he left behind with orders to knock loudly each quarter hour until the door was opened.

At the inn, Beadle sat impatiently, sipping the rare Canary wine he'd brought and waiting for word that MacTeague would see him. No word came. His servant returned after dark, knuckles torn from pounding against the rough planks of the master's portal.

On the third day, when again Beadle's knocks went unanswered, the big, round, and red-faced merchant descended into the glen itself. He found MacTeague beneath a great elm, watching Merton the Quiet swinging a driver.

"Be ye MacTeague?" Beadle shouted.

The master ignored him, intent upon Merton's efforts.

"Be ye MacTeague?" the rich man repeated.

Merton turned to stare, and MacTeague followed his glance. "Ye've disturbed the boy," he chided.

"I've come to learn golf," Beadle announced.

"Good," the master allowed. "But not here."

"I want *you* to teach me."

"I do not teach *people*," replied MacTeague, not moving from under his tree. "I teach golf."

"And that's what I've come to learn," Beadle declared. "I want to play golf."

"We do not *play* golf here."

"Not play golf?" the merchant shrieked. "Am I not blind? I see the lad with a club in his hands."

"We do not *play* golf," MacTeague repeated, turning now to study his visitor more carefully. "We practice it."

"Practice or play, it's all the same to me."

"Aye, that's likely."

Beadle would not be deterred. He argued, cajoled, and tried even to bribe the master of Frither Glen. "Ye be the best that teach, and I will have none other."

Finally, MacTeague seemed to relent. "I will give one lesson. And it will pain me. But not so much as 'twill pain ye, for I keep a hard school.

The merchant was delighted.

" 'Twould be better," warned the master, "to go elsewhere. Let others teach ye enough of the game to play and maybe find some joy in it. Ye'll not have that from me. Stay, and I'll turn ye away from golf."

Beadle would not be swayed.

"Then follow me," ordered MacTeague, rising and striding swiftly down the glen toward the gentle stream that curved across the valley. He stopped by the bank, took a handful of balls from Merton and threw them into the mud. He took a second handful, a third, a fourth, and more, until full 50 yards of bank were marked by balls embedded every foot or more. "Now," he commanded, thrusting a club at Beadle, "hit them free and bring them to me."

"How do I place my hands?" Beadle asked, taking the club. "Are ye not supposed to show me that first, and how to place my feet and draw the club head back?"

"See how much he knows already," beamed the master, turning to Merton. "He knows we've special ways to place our hands and feet and draw back the club head."

"But I don't know which way," complained the rich man.

"Show me what ye can do, and I'll tell ye how. But strike away, man, the balls are waiting."

Beadle stepped gingerly onto the bank, wary of soiling his fine leather shoes. He grasped the club like an ax and swung down hard at the ball. A clod of mud flew up from the bank and spatterings marked his rich breeches. He swung again, and again. Finally, he hit the ball, driving it deeper into the mud.

"Good," said MacTeague, "but the feet must be set down firm. Ye'll hit no balls upon yer toes."

With a grimace, Beadle set his heels down and struck on. In time, he lifted a ball. Later, another. The master applauded each success.

After two hours, half the balls had been moved and Beadle was covered with mud. Still, he kept at it. He was rewarded, from time to time, with a word from MacTeague. "Left arm, 'tis the left arm that swings the club" or "Like a bird, ye hold the club. Too tight and ye smother it. Too loose and it flies away."

It was well past noon, when the last ball had cleared the bank. A grim but determined Beadle gathered them and brought them to MacTeague. "Now," said the master, "come along." He marched briskly up from the stream to a thick stand of brier. Taking the balls from the merchant, he threw them one by one into the thorny bushes. Beadle's face paled. MacTeague smiled. "Hit them out."

The merchant paused, then plunged into the tangle. Thorns scratched his face and arms. They ripped his shirt and snagged his breeches. He swung twice before striding out again to confront MacTeague. "How do ye expect I can hit a ball in there?"

"I don't," the master admitted.

"Then why, in God's name, should I try?"

" 'Tis golf," MacTeague explained.

"No, 'tis not," Beadle shouted. "Golf is hitting the ball from tee to hole."

"Ye want me to teach that?"

"I do."

"But I teach all of golf," MacTeague said quietly. "Any ninny can show ye to hit off a tee or fine, thick grass. Learning to make the shots ye can make, any fool can do. But learning to bear the shots ye cannot make, that's what's hard. That's what I teach."

Beadle was bested. He argued and wheedled some more, but his heart was not in it, and he was far from Frither Glen when night fell.

Merton the Quiet was uneasy, for he had witnessed all of the merchant's lesson, so different from his own first session with the master. "Why?" he asked.

"I must teach a man," said MacTeague, "what he needs to learn."

"'Tis golf," MacTeague explained.

23 THE 18 IDEAL DOUBLE BOGEY HOLES IN AMERICA

FEW GOLF COURSES are consciously designed for Double Bogey Golfers. (The exception is the special layout on Medford Redford's Puget Sound estate, included here *in toto* as the back nine of the Ideal Double Bogey Course.) The following holes are those most suited to our special, limited skills, although not all should be played in the manner envisaged by their designers.

■   ■   ■

■ NO. 1 ■

The seventh hole at Omaha's Deep Dish Country Club (par four, 327 yards) is a right dogleg. The tee faces Deep Dish Ravine, and any drive that exceeds 164 yards is forever lost in the vastness below. Using a five, six, or seven wood, the player should aim for a point 30 to 40 yards beyond the canyon cliff toward the center of the fairway. A moderate slice will carry his ball alongside the right rough. A normal slice or mild shank with a five, six, or seven iron will propel the ball up close to the green. However, the golfer who attempts to place his second shot on the green will most frequently (77 percent of the time) succeed only in reaching the right bunker.

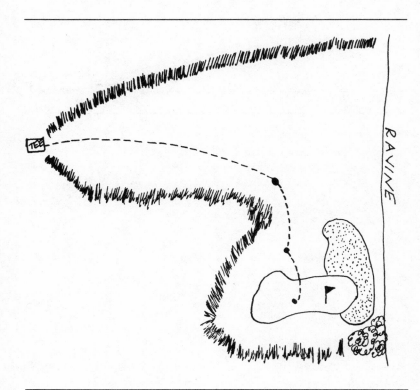

■ NO. 2 ■

The 16th hole at Derry Derry Downs (par four, 410 yards) runs straight downhill from tee to green (a drop of 137 feet in elevation) with the fairway banked high on either side. Shoving off the tee with a four, five, or six iron, the Double Bogey Golfer should fly his ball some 70 yards or more and watch it roll an additional 135 yards before coming to rest. A second shot, similar to the first, will place the ball either on or directly in front of the green.

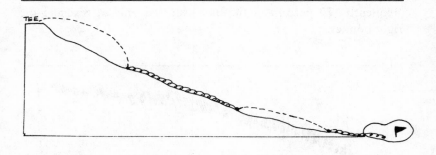

■ NO. 3 ■

The third (and final) hole of Middleville, Montana's Downtown
Golfing Promenade (par five, 472 yards) starts straight down
Fourth Street to Veteran's Park. Any drive from the tee in front of
Bosworth's Department Store will bound the length of the street to
the park grass. A bobble of no more than 50 yards will then put it
into position to be bounced the length of Main Street and onto the
green in City Hall Plaza. Although it is not recommended, the
golfer with a high, reliable slice may choose to play up and over
Bosworth's. If so he may hope for the birdie, but he must be prepared to pay the price of his ambition. The interior of the store,
including the sports department, is out of bounds.

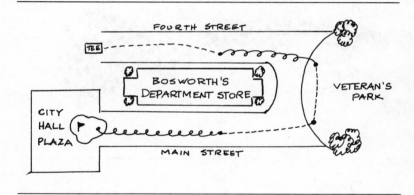

▪ NO. 4 ▪

The 12th hole at Wheeling's Rushes Ho Hotel (par five, 465 yards) circumscribes a small woods. Four middling slices with a short wood or midiron will place the Double Bogey Golfer's ball within a longish putt or short scull of the green. More skillful players usually avoid the fairway completely and play a wedgewood from the right side of the tee, across a narrow band of trees between tee and green. A near-certain double bogey for the steady Double Bogey Golfer, the hole normally produces an eagle for lower-handicap players.

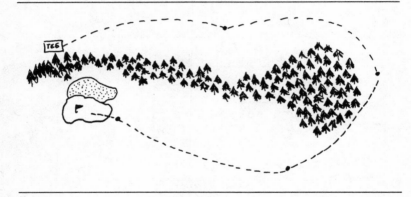

▪ NO. 5 ▪

The eighth hole at Blasted Heath, near Stonington, Connecticut (par three, 137 yards), is usually played straight across the pool of this former granite quarry. However, the sheer cliffs on each side of the hole give the Double Bogey Golfer a rare opportunity to make the green with his initial shot. Sliced with a low-numbered wood into a spot on the right cliff wall (marked by a patch of blue paint) approximately 60 yards from the tee, the ball will carom across the pool to the left wall and rebound from there to the green or the open fairway on its right.

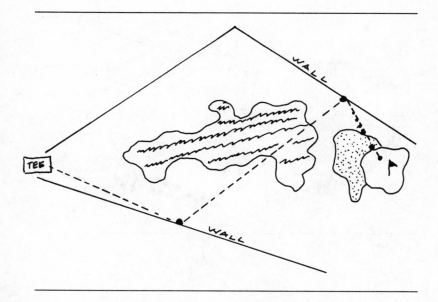

▪ NO. 6 ▪

The 10th hole at Hemlock Cups (par four, 385 yards) crosses Interstate 95 on the right flank of Hemlock Hill. A weak to moderate drive of 130 to 145 yards should strike the road and bound an extra 50 yards or so down the fairway. The second shot should never be played straight for the hole, since it will land in deep woods if sliced. Instead, the Double Bogey Golfer must aim well to the left, using a six or seven iron to reach the steep slope from which the ball will roll directly to the green.

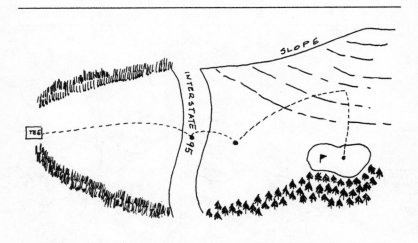

▪ NO. 7 ▪

The only hole at the Incredible Living Singles Residence and Recreation Center in Detroit starts on the roof and drops 16 stories to a green beside the swimming pool. Any club, stroked in moderation, may be used from the tee.

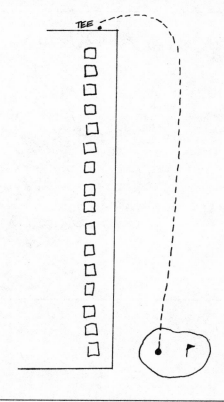

▪ NO. 8 ▪

The eighth at Purple Sage (par four, 422 yards) is a conventional right dogleg. However, the Double Bogey Golfer should avoid the fairway and take the direct route from tee to green along a 233-yard culvert. The green can be reached in three strokes and several thousand bounces.

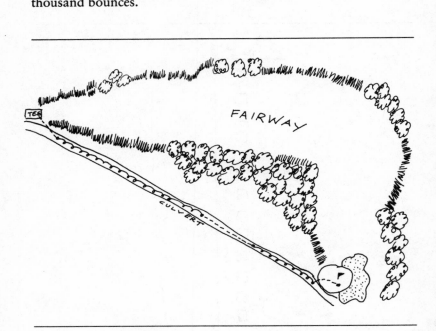

▪ NO. 9 ▪

The fourth hole at Cold Charity (par five, 531 yards) drops into a ravine and swings left on the slope below the clubhouse. Ignoring the fairway, the Double Bogey Golfer should play a seven or eight iron for the far left corner of the parking lot. Taking a one-stroke penalty for an unplayable ball, he must launch his second shot from alongside the first tee. With a five or seven iron, he should easily reach the green.

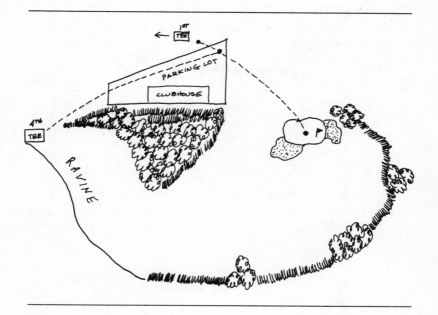

▪ NOS. 10–18 ▪

Medford Redford has pushed golf a long stride forward by creating the ideal nine-hole Double Bogey course at his estate on Puget Sound. Situated at the top of a vast slope near the sea, a single tee overlooks a vista of nine separate greens. The holes are untrapped and unnumbered and may be played in any sequence a golfer chooses. In fact, the same hole may be played twice, but not in succession. No mulligans are permitted on Redford's course, but it is unlikely that a player's initial drive will land far from at least one of the greens.

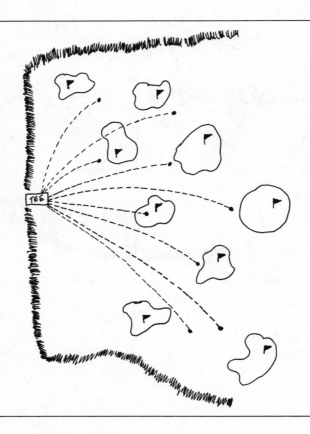

24 ZEN AND THE ART OF THE DOUBLE BOGEY GOLFER

Vanity of vanities, Qoheleth says. All is vanity. For all his toil under the sun, what does man gain by it?

ECCLESIASTES 1:2–3

THE DOUBLE BOGEY Golfer is not a quitter. And the more optimistic ones never cease to seek the way, the path of enlightenment that leads to a lower handicap. Fortunately, their search often brings them into contact with the ancient Chinese philosophers. One such wise man once remarked, perhaps apropos of the favored sport: "If the wrong man uses the right means, the right means work in the wrong way." Properly meditated upon, much can be learned from this saying.

Through Zen, which is Chinese Buddhism with a Japanese name, we can enter the realm of mystical paradox, which is where we are anyway when we play golf. The great Zen teachers took a puckish glee in confounding those who sought their advice. One of their favorite ploys was to ruminate for a goodly period, and then simply answer a question with another question.

As an instance, the famed Joshu was asked what he would give a poverty-stricken peasant who came to him. He replied: "What is wanting in him?" The fellow who asked the question hung around for a while, but that was all he got.

Another time, Joshu was asked, "When a man comes to you with nothing, what would you say to him?" This time he answered without hesitation: "Cast it away!"

One devotee of Zen golf took the answer to apply to his pitching wedge, which never responded the way it was supposed to. Another thought that what was meant was the game itself; he promptly took up tennis.

Important to remember about Zen, however, is that one of its primary purposes is to baffle the logically trained intellect. "Cast it away!" then, must not be taken in any literal sense. By digging beneath the paradox, we can interpret the saying to mean: Allow the mind and body to float over the great fairways of nothingness.

The mystically inclined golfer will find this particularly helpful if he realizes that the Zen teacher is not concerned with lowering anyone's handicap. Rather, it is a beatific state of being that he aims, in his seemingly puzzling way, to help us advance toward.

So it was that the great Ummon stated: "In Zen there is absolute freedom; sometimes it negates and at other times it affirms; it does either way at pleasure."

Isn't this a paradigm of what so often happens in Double Bogey Golf? On occasion a five-iron shot will head unerringly for a bunker; virtually the same shot, on the same course, on another day, will stop four feet short of the pin. Has not this happened to all of us?

A monk (Japanese) pondered Ummon's words and asked him: "How does it negate?"

Ummon answered: "With the passing of winter there cometh spring."

Elliptical perhaps, but well said! A winter of inactivity, during which the muscles unlearn all the wrong things they have been doing, is followed by the new season. Miraculously, that nagging slice has straightened in the interim.

The monk, though, persisted, asking Ummon: "What happens when spring cometh?"

Ummon, perhaps weary of the monk, answered with unusual lucidity. "Carrying a staff across the shoulders, let him ramble about the fields and beat the old stumps to the heart's content."

In Japan, those words have echoed through history, and are even to be found in a book of classic haiku, as follows:

ツエを背に、野をさまよい歩き 自然を思いっきり楽しむ

Akira Hawakaya, a student of Zen, who plays the Osaka Country Club course, and who was runner-up in its 1989 Class E tournament, was kind enough to supply us with what he feels is the contemporary interpretation of Ummon's noted saying: "Be content with your 32 handicap; enjoy the intoxicating odors of moist earth and sprouting blades of grass, of bird song, and of unpolluted air."

It was also Hawakaya who apprised us of the fact that one of the greatest of Zen teachers, Wopei, actually played golf. His pronouncements on the game, dating from the 17th century, gained such fame that they came to the attention of MacTeague, the Sage of Frither Glen, who thereupon invited him to Scotland for a friendly twosome. Wopei, according to Hawakaya, took a roundabout route, stopping first at the hut of Shuzan, in a remote region of Tibet.

It was there, as he observed Shuzan in his practice swings on the first tee of a six-hole course fashioned from a former goat pasture, that Wopei remarked in rhymed couplet:

> *By the castle of the king of Ch'u*
> *Eastward flows the stream of Ju.*

Shuzan, who hitherto had never managed to play the six holes in less than 47, suddenly shot an astounding 36. After that, long after

Wopei's departure, Shuzan, during practice swings, never failed to repeat the couplet:

> *By the castle of the king of Ch'u*
> *Eastward flows the stream of Ju.*

And his scores invariably ranged between 35 and 37. No one, not even Shuzan, knew why the couplet proved so efficacious. To this day, little children in that region of Tibet sing the song at their play, little realizing that it was Wopei's contribution to the game of golf.

Wopei, it is said, continued onward, with brief stops in Persia, Corsica, Switzerland, and Holland (where the game at the time was still called "gowff"), scattering sayings along the way, not all of them, unfortunately, preserved. Some, however, have survived and can be found in the Japanese volume, *The Gorfing Travels of the Sage Wopei.* "Gorfing," by the way, is not a misprint. The Japanese of the period did call the game "gorf," perhaps for phonetic reasons.

An odd event, not without its significance, occurred when Wopei played the water hole (the fourth) at Apeldoorn in Holland. His niblick shot plopped into Ossfeld Pond. Meditatively, Wopei watched the spreading ripples made by the ball, then hummed a cheerful little tune: "Ting-ting, tung-tung, ku-ti, ku tung!"

The other members of his foursome (all Dutch) marveled at his composure in the face of disaster. Their shots, too (it was a double bogey foursome), landed in the pond, and each one, following Wopei's example, then hummed the same words to the same tune. Cheerful, laughing, filled with love for the game, they swallowed their penalties with nary their customary curses.

It is now traditional at Apeldoorn to hum that tune when anyone lands in Ossfeld Pond, and new members are required to memorize it before being given access to the course.

Eventually, Wopei arrived at Frither Glen. Easterly autumn winds had come from seaward; gorse and brambles had made the rough of the links all but impenetrable. Nevertheless, the match took place. There is said to be an account of the epic struggle written by a reporter for the *Glasgow Golfing Chronicle,* a periodical now defunct, its files burned for fuel during the winter of 1749. Luckily, some of the verbal exchanges are to be found in *The Gorfing Travels of the Sage Wopei,* again supplied through the good graces of Hawakaya.

On the very first tee, Wopei hooked his drive into a thick bramble patch 80 yards from the tee.

"So," growled MacTeague, when it was apparent the ball was lost, "the rules are firm. You may take three paces in any direction but forward, and drop a new ball over the left shoulder. You will be hitting three."

Wopei gave him an inscrutable smile and said: "The spade is in my hands, and yet empty-handed I go."

Whereupon he mashed his next shot in a slicing arc that caught a wandering cow in the rump and dropped directly beneath its udders.

"Ho ho," laughed MacTeague, "and how will you play from there?"

Wopei merely shrugged, saying: "Who is he who has no companion among the 10,000 things of the world?"

The laird of Frither Glen was among the gallery, and he gave a ruling. Unless the cow moved of its own volition, the ball must be played from where it lay. Five minutes were allowed before Wopei was required to make the shot.

When the five minutes had elapsed and the cow had not moved, Wopei climbed on the back of the beast, his cleek in hand. "I walk on foot," he told the onlookers, "and yet on the back of an ox I am riding." At that moment the cow, having finished her cud, moved to another patch of grass. Nonplussed, the laird of Frither Glen and MacTeague wondered how to rule on this new development.

Wopei came up with the answer: "When I pass over the bridge, lo, the water floweth not, but the bridge doth flow."

"No penalty," promptly ruled the laird, much to MacTeague's discomfiture.

Apparently the match ended in a tie, for it was not recorded in the annals as either a victory or loss for MacTeague, nor does the

Gorfing Travels mention the outcome. What that classic does record, however, are the farewell remarks made by MacTeague and Wopei.

"May I offer the great sage a nip of the spirited stuff?" asked MacTeague.

"One who understands Zen," replied Wopei, "has already attained to the spiritual essence."

"Then you have no need of our national spirits?"

In answer to this, Wopei recited the mantrum: "Om o-lo-lok-kei-svaha!"

"I do not understand," said MacTeague.

"Nor do I," said Wopei, and took his leave.

MacTeague spent many weeks, according to tradition, pondering those last words of Wopei, at length deciding that not to understand *is* to understand. His clue came from an acquaintance with the philosophy of the *Kena-Upanishad,* not dissimilar to Zen, but one which makes no attempt to explain the mystical ways of golf.

The *I ching,* one of six ancient Taoist classics, and known as the Book of Changes, has also proven helpful for Double Bogey Golfers. From the third century B.C. onward, Chinese oracles have made divinations and foretellings based on the *I ching* appendixes (of which it largely consists) and its linear symbols, the hexagrams. Many of the interpretations were based on those two primal forces of nature known as the yin and the yang.

Briefly stated, yang is the male principle, representing the sun, activity, the positive, the right. Yin, as the female principle, represents the moon, quiescence, the negative, the left. When these forces are not in balance, problems result. Too much yang, and the golfer will slice; too much yin, and the golfer will hook. Predominantly yang golfers drive farther than yin golfers, but land more frequently in the rough. Yin golfers tend to hit into bunkers. Paul Azinger is said to represent an equable distribution of the two opposing forces.

The more mystically inclined among golfers have found solace in the hexagrams and their interpretations. One such is number six, also known as the Sung Hexagram, because it was Sung's interpretation that was regarded as the classic one. Herewith is the Sung Hexagram:

Sung may well have been a golfer of the double bogey variety, for he intimates through the hexagram how, though there is sincerity in one's contention, he will yet meet with opposition and obstruction. He goes on to suggest that by cherishing an apprehensive caution, there will be good fortune. Surely this applies to one of our own tenets: Play the par four for a six, and you might wind up with a five. But in that hexagram, Sung finds a warning. "If he must prosecute the contention to the bitter end, there will be evil." Thus, he would seem to be advocating the use of a seven or nine iron out of the rough rather than the more reckless four wood.

The Double Bogey Golfer should study the *I ching,* as well as the *Li chi* (the Book of Rites, or Rituals) and the *Shu ching* (Book of History, or Records). Nor should he overlook the *Midrashim* of the ancient Hebrew teachers, preserved most authentically in the Babylonian Talmud. There are many other mystical sources to be culled by the Double Bogey Golfer in search of enlightenment. Zoroastrianism, the teachings of Ishtar, the secrets of the Druids, Rosicrucianism—from all these the Double Bogey Golfer can gain comfort and help. But certain things are taboo. It is dangerous to consult texts on Egyptian magic and medieval alchemy, nor should he attempt arcane rites or the use of exorcism. These have been known to raise demons and other evil spirits that inhabit golf balls during an entire season. Some even inhabit the golfer. There was the case of Bodinz von Haralyi, who turned into a wolf on the 14th hole at Bad Badingaden. But that is another story.

There are many . . . mystical sources to be culled by the Double Bogey Golfer in search of enlightenment.

25 A LOOK INTO THE FUTURE OF THE WIDE, WIDE WORLD OF DOUBLE BOGEY GOLF

IT WAS ONLY to be expected that sooner or later Double Bogey Golfers would want their share of the television spotlight. With golf tournaments proliferating for professional men, women, juniors, and seniors, as well as for amateur men, women, juniors, and seniors, and this cup and that cup, it was time to remedy a serious neglect.

Double Bogey Golfers banded together, importuned the USGA and the networks, and the result was the First Nationally Televised Double Bogey Golf Tournament, held in April 1995 at the Shifty Sands Country Club near Las Vegas, Nevada. The last of the four exciting rounds was covered live by the NBC network, with a prestigious threesome of Jack Nicklaus, Lee Trevino, and Greg Norman as commentators. The remarks that follow were extracted from the videotape ($89.95 at your local pro shop) of the final three holes of the event:

NICKLAUS: Well, here we are at the 16th hole of Shifty Sands, and I'd say it was anyone's tournament at this point. Do you agree, Greg and Lee?

NORMAN: Oh, yes, definitely, Jack, with the possible exception of Monty Micklehoot, who has just taken 14 strokes on the 14th. Sorry to have to tell you that he sent four straight tee shots into the water, and three more out of the trap at the left of the green.

TREVINO: I don't think he's out of it, Greg. Let's see, he's 120 over par at this point, which puts him only eight strokes back, with four to play. Anything can happen in Double Bogey Golf. If he can stay out of traps and get that ginty of his working, I'd say he has a chance.

NICKLAUS: It's certainly a free-for-all right now, with Kaftenbach, Beltscher, Gorelik tied for the lead at 112 over par. Shh . . . Kaftenbach is at the tee of the 16th, a neat little par four of 286 yards with a dogleg to the right. Can you see the club he's taking, Lee?

TREVINO: An interesting choice—4½ wood. He's hoping to clear the 100 yards of rough before the fairway.

NORMAN: He made it! And with two or three yards to spare. How would you describe Kaftenbach's swing, Jack?

NICKLAUS: I'd rather not, Greg. Meanwhile, Beltscher's at the tee. My God! Forgive the expletive, folks, but I've never seen a swing like that before.

NORMAN: Almost impossible to describe—not for what they're paying me for this job. (Uneasy "ha ha.")

TREVINO: I'll give it a try. . . . He takes the club back in what I'd call exaggerated slow motion, looks up at the sky, down at his toes, clenches his teeth and his grip, bends his knees, stands upright, seems to be praying, then . . .

NICKLAUS: Sorry to interrupt, Lee, but it appears his ball has found the heavy rough after dribbling 50 yards from the tee. He'll need a shovel to get out of that stuff.

TREVINO: To finish my description of Beltscher's swing, he holds out his little finger on his right hand . . .

NORMAN: Shh . . . Boomer Gorelik is hitting.

NICKLAUS: What a hit! As long a ball as any today, something like 250 yards and one of the most remarkable slices I've ever seen, way over there toward the 15th tee. Trouble is, he's made the hole twice as long to play.

TREVINO: His ball has hit someone, Jack.

NORMAN: Yes, the Boomer's ball hit Micklehoot, on the tee of the 15th. Oh, is he mad! Claiming foul. Says Gorelik did that deliberately. Seems they have this ongoing nassau . . .

NICKLAUS: I happen to know Gorelik personally, and regard him as one of the finest gentlemen in Double Bogey Golf. In fact, I've offered to work with him on his slice.

TREVINO: He told me he faces 90 degrees left of center, and it still happens.

NICKLAUS: That's the whole point. I'd face him 90 degrees to the right. It's worth a try anyway.

NORMAN: The tournament director has just ruled no foul. In Double Bogey Golf, it's up to the fellow on the tee to watch out for himself for what happens on other holes.

NICKLAUS: Time to break for a commercial, fellows. Don't go away, folks. Take my word for it—there are fireworks ahead.

(Commercial Break)

NICKLAUS: We're back at Shifty Sands for our coverage of the First Nationally Televised Double Bogey Golf Tournament. We're on the final few holes, and word has just reached us that Monty Micklehoot has done the all but impossible. He has *parred* the 15th!

NORMAN: Only the second par of the entire tournament, Jack.

TREVINO: He stays at 120 over, and I'd say he's definitely in it. Especially with the ruling made on Gorelik's long slice from the 16th tee to the 15th tee. After hitting Micklehoot, the ball landed on the cart path, which marks the boundary. Right now he's in the rough on the 17th, which parallels the 16th. In trying to hit a hook, he faced almost backward. He hit the hook all right, but look where he is. He's got to get over those high cacti and the bunker beyond. Wowee! The excitement is mounting.

NICKLAUS: Word is in on Micklehoot's amazing par on the 15th. His third shot hit a power line and the ball fell straight down into a bunker 40 yards from the green. He managed to scuff the ball out; it bounced off a hillock guarding the green, and bobbled into the hole. We've got instant replay on it. That commotion you see is after Micklehoot fainted. He's definitely okay now. His caddy gave him a shot of something. I know he likes Southern Comfort.

TREVINO: The kids are watching, Jack.

NICKLAUS: Just kidding, Lee.

NORMAN: Whatever it is, his caddy took a swig, too. I suppose the strain is telling on them both. Now he's passing it around. They're applauding. That Micklehoot is a crowd favorite.

TREVINO: Watch his swing. Who's he remind you of, Jack?

NICKLAUS: Ivan Lendl?

TREVINO: Don't mean to correct you, Jack, but he looks to me more like Jimmy Connors. The same fierce concentration.

NORMAN: I admire his attitude. He'll stay on the courts until he's 60.

NICKLAUS AND TREVINO: Courts?

NORMAN: Weren't you talking about Connors?

NICKLAUS: Micklehoot.

NORMAN: Oh. His swing reminds me of McEnroe.

TREVINO: Uh, oh . . . Kaftenbach's made the bunker at the left of the 16th green.

NORMAN: His next shot will be interesting.

NICKLAUS: Why do you say that, Greg?

NORMAN: Watch what he does.

TREVINO: Well, I'll be. . . . He turned around and played it back to the fairway.

NORMAN: Yes, he'll attempt to chip up from there and settle for a seven. Smart play. A few extra strokes don't mean much in this tournament.

TREVINO: I'm told Beltscher boomed his tee shot 160 yards. He's on the fairway, while Gorelik is now in the right rough. That man can hit a ball, but his problem is direction.

NORMAN: In his case, that's quite a problem!

NICKLAUS: Time for another commercial, fellows.

(Commercial Break)

NICKLAUS: Here we are at the 17th at Shifty Sands Country Club, par 70, 5,600 yards in length. It's a most difficult course, especially designed for the Double

Bogey Golfer to present them with the kind of difficulties they're prone to encounter. Greg, you played this course once in an exhibition. How'd you do?

NORMAN: Badly. I kept overdriving the green.

TREVINO: On the par fours?

NORMAN: And the fives.

NICKLAUS: This is the way we stand. Kaftenbach and Beltscher are tied for the lead at 115 over par, and Gorelik is a stroke back at 116. Meanwhile, Micklehoot is thrilling the crowd with his driving finish. He has just bogeyed the 16th, after his fantastic par on the 15th. He's now at 123 over, with two holes to play.

TREVINO: He made the green in four strokes about 100 feet from the pin. He has this unique putting style. He runs his hand along the shaft and sort of bunts the ball.

NORMAN: It went for the hole as if it had eyes. He doesn't fold under pressure. I admire his attitude.

TREVINO: He fainted again, though.

NICKLAUS: He's back on his feet and looks fine. Happy, in fact.

NORMAN: Why shouldn't he be after that bunt . . . uh, putt.

TREVINO: Or whatever's in that bottle.

NICKLAUS: This 17th is the key hole, I think—a par three, with a 110-yard carry over water. Yep, it's happened. Kaftenbach is in the drink.

NORMAN: Gorelik's safe. He sliced back onto the 16th fairway. From there, a hook should take him to the green.

TREVINO: Wait a minute. Wait a minute! They're ruling Gorelik out of bounds. He'll have to hit from the tee again. Beltscher and Kaftenbach, too. They're all hitting three!

NICKLAUS: Know what I'm thinking, Lee and Greg? If these Double Bogey Golf tournaments catch on . . .

TREVINO: I know what you're thinking. We could lose the audience for the pro and senior tours. Maybe we've parred and birdied ourselves to death. Nothing unexpected, all those predictable shots, perfect look-alike swings. We hit the fairways, hit the greens, get down in two from bunkers, and boredom is bound to set in for the audience.

NORMAN: As long as we have a future as commentators, I'm happy.

NICKLAUS: Beltscher's back in the water.

TREVINO: Oh, oh, so is Kaftenbach.

NORMAN: Gorelik has hit his shot a mile high, but it's straight, absolutely straight . . .

TREVINO: . . . into the water.

NICKLAUS: We'll have to leave them there for the moment. Commercial time.

(Commercial Break)

NICKLAUS: We're back at Shifty Sands for the 18th hole of the fourth and final round of the First Nationally Televised Double Bogey Golf Tournament, limited to players who have never broken 100. The competition is keen, and has produced some truly astounding shot making. Beltscher and Kaftenbach took quadruple bogeys on the 17th, while Gorelik settled for a triple. That puts all three at a tie for the lead at 119 over par. Meanwhile Micklehoot has just achieved another bogey on the 17th, placing him two strokes back at 121. They tell me the Micklehoot charge is well known in Double Bogey Golf circles.

TREVINO: You know something? I don't think there's been this much golf excitement since Bobby Jones completed his Grand Slam at Merion in 1930.

NORMAN: And we have an interesting situation here. Kaftenbach, Beltscher, and Gorelik are all on the green of this par five in five strokes each, in good position to make their par—that is, double bogeys. And Micklehoot's third shot has just landed some 80 yards from the green. Gorelik is putting now, an 18 footer.

NICKLAUS: The ball slides past the hole about six feet.

TREVINO: Kaftenbach's turn. Nice putt. Three feet from the hole.

NORMAN: If Beltscher makes his . . . 12 feet, absolutely straight. No break at all.

NICKLAUS: The pressure got to him. He barely touched the ball, and he's still 10 feet away.

NORMAN: Beltscher is still away. His knees are shaking, and his caddy has been allowed to hold them while he putts. Good one. Dead on. It rims the hole and . . . no, it stayed out.

TREVINO: Gorelik misses his six footer. . . . Oh my, he's snapping his putter in half! The tournament officials are conferring with him. The ruling is, since he doesn't have another putter in his bag, he must putt out with what he's got left. He's down on his knees . . . and makes the putt!

NICKLAUS: Kaftenbach has an easy three footer. If he makes it, he has the tournament. It's in! No, it's out! Popped right out of the hole. He's yelling at someone. Claims a photographer snapped his camera just as he stroked the ball. Won't do him a bit of good. I've been through the same situation many times.

NORMAN: All three have triple bogeys and now we have a three-way tie for the play-off at 122 strokes over par. What are the possibilities of Micklehoot's making a bogey? It would put him in at 122 with the others.

TREVINO: I'd say slim.

NORMAN: If he could, we'd have a four-way tie, and a real shoot-out.

NICKLAUS: I'm told they'll cancel the evening news, and we can stay on through the play-off.

TREVINO: That's the network for you—all heart. Did you know they have three vice presidents who play Double Bogey Golf?

NORMAN: No, that's at CBS.

TREVINO: NBC, too.

NICKLAUS: What club is Micklehoot taking for his shot to the green, Lee?

NORMAN: Seven iron. Has he enough club, Jack?

NICKLAUS: Eight yards . . . a seven should do it. Here it comes, a high shot. It's hitting the fringe of the green, rolling down toward the bunker on the left. No, it's stopped short, in heavy rough. How he'll get out of that, I don't know. Isn't he lying four now, Greg.

NORMAN: That's right. Four. Now, if he can get his next shot close . . .

TREVINO: Fifteen thousand awed spectators surrounding this green and you can hear a pin drop. What club is that he's selecting, Jack?

NICKLAUS: Sand wedge. He's looking at his caddie.

TREVINO: Yes, he's getting signals from his caddy. He's touching his cap, slapping his right thigh, and plucking at his shirt.

NORMAN: You Yanks. You have caddies at the bases in your baseball game, don't you?

NICKLAUS: Yes, Greg. Here it comes. Oh my, he's sculled it. A shrieking liner right at the flag. Where's the ball, Lee?

TREVINO: It's caught in the flag, I think. It's not coming down.

NORMAN: The tournament director says he's got 30 seconds to wait before declaring it a lost ball.

NICKLAUS: Too bad. He's made quite a charge up to this point.

TREVINO: No, wait! The ball's coming out of the flag, it's dropping down the pole, it's hovering right at the edge of the cup and . . . I don't believe it! The ball dropped in! Unbelievable, fantastic, totally unique in golf! That shot will go down in history. An amazing par five, and he's won the tournament.

NORMAN: Micklehoot is down. He fainted again. They're trying to revive him by pouring champagne on his head. He's reaching for the bottle. He's drinking the whole bottle straight down! What a capacity. I doubt we'll be able to talk to him.

NICKLAUS: Just a sidelight, fellows. The other three fainted, too, when they saw Micklehoot's ball drop in. They're being carried to the clubhouse, where, hopefully, when they come out of it, we can get a few words with them.

TREVINO: What a tournament, and we'll hope to bring this kind of excitement to viewers many times from now on.

NORMAN: And what about a Grand Slam for Double Bogey Golf? Now there's a concept. I'll discuss it when I get back to down under.

NICKLAUS: Some sad news, fellows. The network informs me they're canceling the Master's and will put this one on in its place. Golf, they say, has finally entered the modern age of the common man.